GodChicks

Awakened

A 90 DAY DEVOTIONAL

Holly Wagner

Regal

From Gospel Light
Ventura, California, U.S.A.

Published by Regal
From Gospel Light
Ventura, California, U.S.A.
www.regalbooks.com
Printed in the U.S.A.

Library of Congress Cataloging-in-Publication Data
Wagner, Holly.
Godchicks awakened : wake up, be brave, and make a difference
in your world / Holly Wagner.
p. cm.
ISBN 978-0-8307-5750-3 (trade paper)
1. Christian women—Religious life. 2. Devotional calendars. I. Title.
BV4527.W29476 2010
242'.643—dc22
2010049864

Rights for publishing this book outside the U.S.A. or in non-English lan-
guages are administered by Gospel Light Worldwide, an international not-
for-profit ministry. For additional information, please visit www.glww.org,
email info@glww.org, or write to Gospel Light Worldwide, 1957 Eastman
Avenue, Ventura, CA 93003, U.S.A.

To order copies of this book and other Regal products in bulk quantities,
please contact us at 1-800-446-7735.

Using stories, humor and the Word of God, Holly Wagner encourages you to pray, serve and persevere your way into God's plan for your life. If you want to become a woman who defends the outcast, marks her path, and engages the promises of God . . . this book will show you how!

Lisa Bevere
Author and Speaker, Messenger International

This book will do just as its title indicates: awaken women of all ages to a deeper awareness of our great God and the amazing way He has fashioned us for His purposes. Using stories from everyday life along with biblical references, Holly has given us another incredibly powerful, practical and life-changing devotional!

Janet Conley
Senior Pastor, Cottonwood Church

In an honest and igniting way, Holly Wagner spends 90 days challenging us to awaken our hearts. In a generation that is being lulled to sleep by our apathy, our distractions and the pains of our past, she reminds us that the only way we will ever reach our potential is to live this life wide awake!

Denise Hildreth Jones
Speaker and Author of *Flying Solo*

Holly Wagner understands that as women of God, we each have a call from Him to make an incredible difference in the world. I know this book will challenge and encourage you to live as a bolder, godlier woman.

Kari Jobe
Worship Leader

Every day, millions of people wake up physically but never fully engage in their activities throughout the day. They are essentially sleepwalking through their lives, missing out on fulfilling their purpose and experiencing the abundant life that Christ has given them. In this devotional, my friend Holly has given us 90 days of sound advice and radical encouragement to help us awaken in every possible way. So wipe your tired eyes, my friend, and don't miss out on one more day. It's time to wake up, and Holly's just the person to help you do it!

Priscilla Shirer
Author and Teacher

Acknowledgments

Thanks to Philip, who once again had conversations with me while I sat behind a laptop writing. Thanks for continuing to be my greatest cheerleader. I love you.

Thanks to Nicole, Ashley and Karla, for your words and your encouragement!

Thanks to the GodChicks at Oasis Church, and the God-Chicks I meet all over the world, for continuing on the journey with me. I couldn't do it without you!!

Thank You, Holy Spirit, for awakening me to a greater purpose, and for equipping me daily to walk it out.

Introduction

"It's time to wake up!"

Did your mom or dad come into your room when you were a child and say that in a loud voice? And did you just want to burrow under your warm covers?

Of course you did. We all like the comfort of sleep.

And yet, it is time to wake up!

It's a new day for each one of us.

It's a new 24-hour day, and it's a new day in the season of our lives as women on planet Earth, at this time in history.

With this new day and this new season comes the responsibility to live life to its fullest potential.

Every daily reading of this devotional will include a Scripture, a thought and a step we can all take to awaken to our potential. And just so you know, this is a grown-up devotional. Not necessarily for women of a certain age, but rather for women who are determined to get up from whatever might be holding them back, take steps toward freedom and then, with courage, help someone else.

We have been awakened from our yesterday.

A yesterday that might have included pain and sorrow.

We are awakened to a future of hope and strength.

We are awakened to our value.

We are awakened to love.

We are awakened to see the need.

We are awakened to be a part of the solution on the planet.

We are awakened to go.

We are awake!

You and I are a part of a company of women dedicated to the cause of Christ; God is using us as His army to fight injustice and bring light to the darkest of places.

Every army has an alarm that sounds when battle is near. It is the sound that awakens the warrior within and gathers the troops.

Perhaps it's time to look at that alarm clock on your nightstand a bit differently. It may just be an alarm of a different kind . . . your call to "rise and shine" for Jesus.

So join me as, together, we wake up to the possibilities before us!

xoxo . . . Holly

Day 1

Get out of bed, Jerusalem! Wake up. Put your face in the sunlight.
God's bright glory has risen for you.
ISAIAH 60:1, *THE MESSAGE*

Nothing feels quite as heavenly as sunshine on your face, especially when you wake up to it after a good night's sleep! Not only does it feel wonderful, but sunshine has a ton of health benefits as well.

Here are just a few:
Prevents illness and disease.
Produces healthy nervous system.
Lowers cholesterol levels.
Makes the heart healthier.
Increases metabolism.
Aids in weight loss. (Woohoo!)
Improves digestion.
Combats depression.

The interesting thing about sunlight is that the benefits listed above are dependent on its usage. Studies show that exposing your face to sunlight for 10 minutes EVERY DAY can provide your body with the Vitamin D that is required for the day. That means if you want the benefits of the sunlight, you have to daily expose yourself to its rays!

The same is true when it comes to our relationship with God. Isaiah 60:1 tells us to "put [our] face in the sunlight. God's bright glory has risen for [us]." We experience God's bright, magnificent glory when we place ourselves in His sunlight. And if we want to get the most out of His magnificent light, we must expose ourselves to it DAILY.

When we spend time every day connecting with God through prayer and reading His Word, we get to soak up all His benefits.

The list is endless, but here are some:
>   Prevents us from being overwhelmed by discouragement.
>   Produces faith, hope and love.
>   Lowers anxiety and worry.
>   Makes our relationships healthier.
>   Increases effectiveness in God's kingdom.
>   Aids in overcoming unforgiveness and bitterness.
>   Improves joy.
>   Combats confusion and uncertainty.

These benefits and more are available today! Don't miss out; go ahead and soak up the sun! ☺

Steps to Awaken

One of the benefits of connecting with God—of placing our face in His sunlight—is that it prevents us from being overwhelmed by fear. Read Psalm 23 today and let His Word bring you peace.

Day 2

ARISE *[from the depression and prostration in which circumstances have kept you—rise to a new life]! Shine (be radiant with the glory of the Lord), for your light has come, and the glory of the Lord has risen upon you!*

ISAIAH 60:1, *AMP* (EMPHASIS ADDED)

arise [*un-rahyz*]—verb—to come into being, action, or notice; originate; appear; spring up.[1]

I have a confession to make . . . I have not always been a morning person. I do my best "rising and shining" after a cup of coffee and some time alone with my Bible and my thoughts.

But rarely in life do we get that kind of easy and quiet start to our day. More often than not, I have awakened to find that my daughter needs last-minute assistance on her science project; my husband can't find his keys (again ☺); the dog needs to get fed; I need to write down notes for an office meeting later in the day; and a friend has left a voicemail during the night about a horrible situation she is going through.

Every now and again, I fantasize about pulling the covers over my head and staying in my warm and cozy bed until noon. Have you ever wanted to do that?

Life might seem a little easier in the comfort of your bed. Sometimes the "work" of the day ahead just seems overwhelming. In this verse in Isaiah, "arise" isn't so much about getting out of bed . . . but rather arising from whatever circumstances would try to keep you down.

I don't know all that is going on in your life, but I would imagine that you might be facing some challenging moments today.

A marriage that has grown stale.
A special-needs child to take care of.
A friend who has betrayed you.
Uncertainty about your career choice.
A tough conversation with a co-worker.

Yep, life would definitely be easier if we could stay in bed. Except for the fact that our God is calling us to rise. The great thing is that He will be with us every moment of this day. Any challenge you encounter today can be faced with His help. There might be some scary situations ahead of you today, but I know you can do it. Don't let the circumstances, or that sense of depression, keep you down. You were born to rise!

Steps to Awaken

• •

Make the decision that whatever challenges are in front of you today . . . you will not be kept down. It really is a decision, not a feeling!

Note
1. s.v. "arise," http://dictionary.reference.com/browse/arise.

Day 3

Therefore He says, Awake, O sleeper, and arise from the dead,
and Christ shall shine (make day dawn) upon you and give you light.
Look carefully then how you walk! Live purposefully and worthily
and accurately, not as the unwise and witless, but as wise (sensible,
intelligent people), making the very most of the time [buying up each
opportunity], because the days are evil.
EPHESIANS 5:14-16, *AMP* (EMPHASIS ADDED)

As a fourth-grader at summer camp, I remember being awakened by a bugle blasting out reveille.

Wow.

Definitely annoying.

And there is not a pillow invented that could block out that sound! But the truth is, whether it is a bugle, a beep, a buzz, ocean waves or a song . . . there is not one alarm sound that I like. I think they are all annoying!

Some days we are awake before the alarm even goes off, because we are excited about what the day might bring. We have no trouble getting out of bed because we are leaving for vacation or going on a first date with someone or it's the first day of school. But eventually, perhaps, the newness of our days wear off, and we need the annoying alarm to get out of bed!

In reality, the sound that wakes me up may not be annoying . . . it is just that I was sleeping so soundly that any noise waking me up would be a bother.

I wonder if that isn't how it is with God's voice? He is trying to wake us up to what is going on in our home, our marriage, our school, our neighborhood, our city, our world; but we don't like the sound of the alarm.

He is trying to wake us up!

But we keep trying to push the snooze button! (Why is it that we even look for a snooze button?? Really, what difference does it make if we get up now or five minutes from now? Just get up!)

I heard one woman talking to another about her marriage. She said that she knew the marriage was in a "not good place." But she just ignored it, and now she has found herself attracted to another man. She ignored the alarm sound and must have kept hitting the snooze button. And now she has real trouble on her hands.

I have heard quite a few people talk about how they "sensed" something was wrong in their body, but they didn't want to go to the doctor. They were a bit afraid of what they might hear and so, in essence, they put the pillow over their head. By the time they did get to the doctor, they had a bigger problem to deal with.

Our God is trying to wake us up, not only because there are things going on in our own lives that need to be dealt with, but also because He has a job for us to do on the planet.

The same alarm clock is ringing all over!
He needs us to wake up.

Steps to Awaken

Make the decision today to quit using the snooze button! Really. Is there something going on in your life that you need to awaken to? Will you trust that your God will be with you as you handle whatever it is?

Day 4

Here's another way to put it: You're here to be light, bringing out the God-colors in the world. *God is not a secret to be kept. We're going public with this, as public as a city on a hill. If I make you light-bearers, you don't think I'm going to hide you under a bucket, do you? I'm putting you on a light stand. Now that I've put you there on a hilltop, on a light stand—shine! Keep open house; be generous with your lives. By opening up to others, you'll prompt people to open up with God, this generous Father in heaven.*

MATTHEW 5:14-16, *THE MESSAGE* (EMPHASIS ADDED)

Why is it that our children generally like to sleep with a light on somewhere? With their eyes closed, it is not like they could see the light . . . but somehow just knowing it is on brings comfort.

Practically speaking, darkness is simply defined as the absence of light.

And darkness isn't darkness anymore when light is revealed.

Jesus says that you and I are here to be light. (Nice to know why we are here!) So maybe as light . . . you and I were created to dispel darkness.

We were created to bring out the "God-colors in the world."

Philip and I like to scuba dive. Initially I thought the goal was to go as deep as possible. While there are some interesting shipwrecks to see at about 150 feet, most of the beauty of scuba diving is found in 30 to 60 feet of water. I remember diving with Philip on one particularly cloudy day. Everything under the water looked gray . . . the coral, the fish and the rocks. All of a sudden the sun made an appearance, and its rays penetrated the water. What had been dull and drab suddenly became radiant with color! I have never seen color like that. The fish looked like Versace had designed them! They were so bright and color-ful! And the coral was spectacular. All of this had been present before the light was there . . . but it remained unseen until the rays of the sun touched it.

Maybe you and I are to bring out the wonder . . . the God-colors . . . that are in the world.

I would imagine that your life, like mine, has some areas that are just a bit boring, a little drab and gray. Rather than feeling frustrated, and disengaging or cursing the darkness . . . maybe you and I are to be the light that brings out the colors. Perhaps we are to add life to a situation.

I have some very dear friends who live in the Seattle, Washing-ton, area. There are some great aspects to that area of the coun-try . . . the coffee being my favorite! However, for most of the year the sky is gray. I guess people just get used to it. (Coming from Southern California . . . the land of perpetual sun . . . I can't imagine it!) While getting used to gray skies is one thing . . . getting used to gray lives is another.

   You and I are here to bring out the color.

Steps to Awaken

Is there an area of your life that is just a bit gray and lifeless? Your marriage, your friendships, your job? What can you do to-day to add some color to this area?

Day 5

"Here's another way to put it: You're here to be light, bringing out the God-colors in the world. God is not a secret to be kept. We're going public with this, as public as a city on a hill. If I make you light-bearers, you don't think I'm going to hide you under a bucket, do you? I'm putting you on a light stand. Now that I've put you there on a hilltop, on a light stand—shine! Keep open house; be generous with your lives. By opening up to others, you'll prompt people to open up with God, this generous Father in heaven.
MATTHEW 5:14-16, *THE MESSAGE* (EMPHASIS ADDED)

In Jesus' day, Palestinian homes generally had one small window and were fairly dark. Interior light usually consisted of a lamp—a bowl filled with oil and a wick. When the house's occupants needed light, they placed the lamp on a lamp stand. The most challenging aspect of having this light in the house was in lighting the lamp. (No matches!)

As a result, no one wanted to let the light go out, because it took too much work to get the wick lit again. However, when people went out of the house it was too dangerous to leave the lamp burning freely. So for safety reasons, when people left their homes, the lamp would be taken from its lamp stand and placed under an earthen vessel where it could burn risk free. As soon as someone returned they would put the lamp on the stand.

Jesus has made us light bearers . . . to shine brightly, not conceal our light under a bucket. And our light is to shine all the time . . . not just when we are feeling good and life is going our way . . . but all the time!

Sometimes, if we let it, our light can shine brightest in our most challenging times.

There were many times in my cancer battle when I was feeling under the weather. When what I wanted to do was stay in bed and pull the covers over my head! Interestingly enough, it was often at these times when I was asked to go speak somewhere, and then end the meeting by praying for the sick. I certainly didn't feel like it! *Hello!* I was dealing with sickness myself . . . and yet, I made the decision . . . more than once, to go and to pray.

We all go through times when it seems like the world is falling down around us. Maybe we have lost a job, or one of our children is making terrible decisions, or a friend has betrayed us or a family member is seriously ill. Sometimes we deal with more than one challenge at a time. I have. And it was painful. It feels dark.

What I know is that the Holy Spirit has given me the strength to not only have peace in navigating the challenge, but to also be a light in someone else's life at the same time.

I don't know where you are or what you might be dealing with at this moment. Maybe you are feeling overwhelmed. I'm sorry. I am still going to ask you to ask God to show you where you can let your light shine.

Steps to Awaken

With your words or a smile or a kind gesture . . . let your light shine today . . . no matter where you are!

Day 6

"Here's another way to put it: You're here to be light, bringing out the God-colors in the world. God is not a secret to be kept. We're going public with this, as public as a city on a hill. If I make you light-bearers, you don't think I'm going to hide you under a bucket, do you? I'm putting you on a light stand. Now that I've put you there on a hilltop, on a light stand—shine! Keep open house; be generous with your lives. By opening up to others, you'll prompt people to open up with God, this generous Father in heaven.

MATTHEW 5:14-16, *THE MESSAGE* (EMPHASIS ADDED)

Have you ever been to an open house?

Real estate agents host them regularly when they are trying to sell a home.

I have walked through many open houses. From the open door to the smiling agent, I feel free to roam through the house. Whether I am interested in the property or not, it is just fun to see inside houses (and eat the refreshments provided!). I have gotten some great decorating ideas as I have walked through these open houses. I especially like walking through model homes where everything is just perfect, and thousands of dollars have been spent in the decorating. I have even taken photos with the idea that maybe I can get my living room to look like the one in the model home! Hasn't happened yet . . . but I live in hope!

I have had an open house at my own house a few times when we were trying to sell it.

Actually, having an open house event was a lot of work. Preparing for hundreds of strangers to walk through my house took effort. Counters needed to be cleared, laundry put away, dishes cleaned, and all clutter, and dog poop, picked up.

I guess people are more apt to buy a clean home!

Jesus is telling us that we need to keep "open house." Perhaps He is saying that we need to live in such a way that our lives are inviting and welcoming to others.

An open-door life.

A welcome-mat-out-front kind of life.

A life where others are free to visit.

I have a friend who always seems to be surrounded by people. She always seems to be open to another friend. And she makes each one feel special and welcome. She is one of the most loving and non-judgmental people I know. She is honest and without guile . . . totally free in who she is. It is so easy to be with her. We don't always agree on everything, and yet I never feel attacked or belittled. Rather than quickly condemning or ridiculing anyone's thoughts, she just listens and loves. She has certainly navigated some challenges . . . an alcoholic father, siblings who have brought so much heartbreak, and an illness that just seems to keep hanging on. She could complain about her life. Many would. But people who are complaining about their hard life are rarely the kind of people that others are drawn to. And she feels the responsibility to live her life in such a way that she can lead people to her Savior. Her "open house" life has drawn many people. Some come just to look, and others come for refreshing. All feel loved.

So how are you doing with living an open-house life? Are you working so hard to protect your heart that you have closed off your life?

Can I ask you to open your heart again? There are people that God will send your way. He is hoping that you will open up to them so that maybe they will open up to Him—our "generous Father in heaven."

Steps to Awaken

Be brave. Ask someone today if she thinks you are an open-house kind of chick. Ask her if she feels welcomed by you.

Day 7

By your words I can see where I'm going;
they throw a beam of light on my dark path.
PSALM 119:105, *THE MESSAGE*

I have spent many hours in airplanes. Looking out from an airplane window at night can be almost magical when the plane is crossing over a city. The twinkling city lights look like a wonderland from thousands of feet overhead. When the plane is preparing to land, I can see the lights on either side of the runway that are present to guide the plane all the way down. I am sure the pilots appreciate those lights. It would be hard to know where to go without them!

I also certainly appreciate my headlights when I am driving at night. Much safer to drive with them on!

Light serves as a guide to help us find our way in the dark.

The psalmist tells us that God's words are a light to our path. Good to know! Have you ever wondered just what to do? Or what step to take? Does the road ahead seem a little dim?

There have been some dark times in my life. Times when the road ahead was dark and I needed some light to find my way through. It was a scary moment when the doctor gave me the diagnosis of cancer. I wasn't sure of all that was to come, but I did know that if I read His Word, clarity would come. So I did.

I will give you back your health and heal your wounds (Jer. 30:17, *NLT*).

He took our sicknesses and removed our diseases (Matt. 8:17, *NLT*).

> He healed every kind of disease and illness (Matt. 4:23, *NLT*).

> And the peace of God, which surpasses all understanding, will guard your hearts and minds through Christ Jesus (Phil. 4:7, *NKJV*).

His Word gave me the peace and the confidence to walk out the path in front of me. This wasn't the first time in my life that I had read those verses; it was just the first time they were my light in the darkness. God teaches us in the light so that we can use it in the dark.

I know where my bedroom furniture is. I learned its placement while it was light. So, at night, I can go to the bathroom without hitting the furniture.

In the light, I learn some things about God, and in the night, I learn some things about me. Faith born in the light is developed in dark moments.

I am not sure where you are today. Maybe you are in the middle of a challenge. Maybe the road ahead looks dark. Let His Word be the light that guides you. Or maybe everything is going great in your world today (good for you!); then use this time to let God teach you with His Word so that you will know it during the challenging parts of your journey.

Steps to Awaken

Find three verses in the Bible that talk about peace. Store them in your heart so that they are there when you need the promise of peace!

Day 8

Then Jesus spoke to them again, saying "I am the light of the world. He who follows Me shall not walk in darkness, but have the light of life."
JOHN 8:12, *NKJV* (EMPHASIS ADDED)

I am sure that most of you have seen a play or performance that required a spotlight to follow one of the performers. A spotlight is often necessary so that our attention is drawn to the performer and so that we can see what is going on.

I live in Los Angeles, which is basically the entertainment capital of the world. While many people move here from around the planet to seek a career either in film, dance or music, some just come looking for the spotlight. There is certainly nothing wrong with wanting to work in the entertainment industry . . . Initially, I moved to Los Angeles with that dream, and for years I made a living doing films and television. The challenge comes when we think the spotlight is for us.

Over the years I have learned that my job is to make God famous—regardless of whatever career or job I might have. It is not my name that brings freedom or healing to anyone, but rather it is His name. Jesus has restored my soul, forgiven my sins, given me a purpose, shown me the way when I was lost, and healed my body. His light has truly shined in my life. But rather than thinking that His light is all for me, I think I am to reflect His light into dark places.

Kind of like a mirror.

His light has shone, and continues to shine, on me . . . but it is not entirely for me. It is so that I can then reflect that light into dark areas.

Areas that need restoration, forgiveness, purpose and healing.

There are people in my world, and people I meet, who need to know His love and His mercy. Maybe my job is to shine that into their lives.

Imagine if we all received His light and then became reflectors of that light . . .

Wow.

Wouldn't be much darkness left, would there?

> Where can I go from your Spirit?
>   Where can I flee from your presence?
> If I go up to the heavens, you are there;
>   if I make my bed in the depths, you are there.
> If I rise on the wings of the dawn,
>   if I settle on the far side of the sea,
> even there your hand will guide me,
>   your right hand will hold me fast.
> If I say, "Surely the darkness will hide me
>   and the light become night around me,"
> even the darkness will not be dark to you;
>   the night will shine like the day,
>   *for darkness is as light to you*
> (Ps. 139:7-12, *NIV,* emphasis added).

I keep thinking about that last verse . . . **darkness is as light to Him.**

You and I are drawn to light. Our attention and eyes would be drawn to any little light in a dark room.

But I wonder if it isn't different with God? His head is turned toward where there might be darkness . . . pain and suffering . . .

loneliness and hurt . . . and He is asking us to be the light . . . to reflect His light.

He is sending us into the world . . . this twenty-first-century world that is filled with immorality, iniquity, crime, violence, greed, heartbreak, pain, and the list goes on . . . and He is saying, "Be the light!"

Steps to Awaken

. . . .

What situation or circumstance in your world requires a little light? How can you be that light?

Day 9

Open your mouth for the dumb [those unable to speak for themselves],
for the rights of all who are left desolate and defenseless; open your
mouth, judge righteously, and administer justice for the poor and needy.

PROVERBS 31:8-9, AMP

In Matthew, chapter 5, Jesus challenged us to keep open house with our lives. What is it about us that should be open?

In Proverbs, we are told that our mouth is to be open.

Some of us were just waiting for someone to give us permission for our mouth to stay open! As women we do have lots of words to say! This is awesome . . . God made us that way! But maybe, just maybe, there is a reason??

I don't think our mouth should be open just to be open.

Our mouth should be open for those who are unable to speak for themselves . . . for those who are left desolate and defenseless . . . to administer justice for the poor and needy.

Justice simply means to make right what has been wrong.

Have there been times when a word from you would have made a situation right? Maybe simply saying, "I'm sorry," "I love you," "I forgive you" or "I believe in you."

I have a friend who, like so many others, was raised in a broken family. She was made to feel like she had to be perfect in order to be loved. So, for years she tried. Every mistake she made was held over her head. Every time she did something wrong, love was withheld. As a young woman, she moved to Los Angeles, and eventually was in my world. On one particular day, when I wasn't around, she accidentally broke something of mine. She was so nervous to tell me, convinced that because of her mistake I would get angry and pull away from her. I had no idea all of this was going through her head. A few hours later, when she told me what she had broken, I simply said, "No big deal ... I do stuff like that all the time." I didn't know until weeks later that my simple, easy words of forgiveness released her first step toward freedom and healing.

Perhaps your child is confused or hurting right now. Your words have the power to make it right.

Are there words you could say to your husband that would make a situation right? (And just a thought, with men ... less is more ... I'm not just talking about clothes!)

There have been so many times when all Philip needed from me to make his day right was an encouraging word, and often what he got was a paragraph of things that needed changing.

Now, I am sure you have never done anything like that!

Or is there a friend who could use the right words from you that will make it right?

Steps to Awaken

What words can you say today that would bring freedom, healing ... or simply release the pressure in someone's life? Open your mouth and say them.

Day 10

When I was a grade-school student, my report card often included the comment:

"Talks too much in class."

I am sure that was true . . . and it probably still is today. I always seem to have something to say, and someone to say it to! I will probably never err on the side of not saying anything . . . but rather on the side of saying too much or saying the wrong thing!

You and I are supposed to open our mouths, but really we are to open them for a reason . . . to make a situation right. On a bigger scale . . . how can we open our mouths and use our voices to help the poor and needy, the down-and-outers?

The orphan and the widow?

The homeless?

The victims of human trafficking?

All who are left desolate and defenseless?

Nancy Alcorn, the founder of Mercy Ministries . . . has become a voice for a generation of young women . . . those who are broken and wounded . . . she has opened her mouth on their behalf. Young, hurting women from all over the world are welcomed into the Mercy homes. They are loved on, taught their value and instructed in how to walk out their freedom. Nancy opened her mouth and made some things right.

Voice of the Martyrs is an organization that seeks to make the world aware of Christians who are imprisoned and tortured for their faith. It might be surprising to some just how many Christians are put in prison simply because they use the name of Jesus. Freedom for those who are imprisoned often comes as a result of thousands of people "opening their mouths" and writing letters. Pretty simple, really.

We can open our mouths in prayer. In so many ways, situations can seem overwhelming . . . in our own lives . . . in our marriages . . . in the lives of our friends going through challenging times. Often we may not know what to say.

And certainly as we read statistics of human trafficking, hunger, injustice, poverty . . . we can think, *What can I do?*

What you can do is open your mouth and pray!!

Prayer engages the God of the Angel-armies!

> Human Trafficking is the fastest growing global crime, and the world has no easy answers or solutions. We believe that as we step out in prayer this year things will begin to shift in the heavenly realms and change will begin to happen in very tangible ways. Prayer is not a last resort, the Bible says that prayer can change nations and heal lands. Prayer is a weapon that we can use to wage wars that look impossible in the natural.[1]

You and I may never see any of those people this side of eternity . . . but we can pray! We can be generous—we can shine our light, open our mouth and pray for their freedom.

Step to Awaken

Pick a country on the Colour Sisterhood prayer map and pray for our sisters who are in bondage. Pray for their comfort, rescue

and freedom (see http://www.thecoloursisterhood.com/nations/
prayermap).

Note

1. "Prayer Map: The Facts," The Colour Sisterhood. http://www.thecoloursister
hood.com/nations/prayermap.

Day 11

*The earnest (heartfelt, continued) prayer of a righteous man makes
tremendous power available [dynamic in its working].*
JAMES 5:16, AMP

There was a time, a number of years ago, when I felt so guilty
about a choice I made in college . . .
   A time when I was confused about the man I was to marry . . .
   A time when my daughter was bitten in the face by a dog and
blood was everywhere . . .
   A time when I had more bills than money . . .
   There was the time when I was writing my first book . . .
   A time when I was diagnosed with a life-threatening disease . . .
   A time when a friend betrayed me . . .
   A time when I was feeling overwhelmed with what I have
been entrusted with . . .
   And right now, my grandfather is on the last pages of his life,
and I am not sure about his relationship with Jesus.

In each of these situations initially, my only response was and
is . . . to cry out to God.

To talk to my heavenly Father.

**The Bible is full of men and women who talked to their God,
and He answered.**

Moses cried out to God, and God spared Israel from judgment.
   Joshua's prayer made the sun stand still.
   Hannah's prayer was answered with the birth of a baby boy.
   Solomon received wisdom in answer to his prayer.
   Peter prayed, and Dorcas rose from the dead.
The real secret to answered prayer is to pray!

A. C. Dixon wrote, "When we rely upon organization, we get what organization can do; when we rely upon education, we get what education can do; when we rely upon eloquence, we get what eloquence can do, and so on. Nor am I disposed to undervalue any of these things in their proper place, but when we rely upon prayer, we get what God can do."[1]

You might have read the book or seen the movie *The Horse Whisperer*, or watched the TV reality show *Dog Whisperer*. In each of these we see someone who learns to understand what the horse or dog is trying to say and then works to speak that language. The person does this in order to build a relationship with the animal.

I just think the most important relationship we can build is with our God, so let's talk to Him! Maybe we should be known as God Whisperers!

Steps to Awaken
· ·

Take a few minutes right now to pray. Pray for a situation in your life in which you need to see the touch of God.

Note
    1. Dr. A. C. Dixon, quoted by Robert Hall Glover, *The Bible Basis of Missions* (Los Angeles, CA: Bible House of Los Angeles, 1946).

Day 12

Is any one of you in trouble? He should pray. Is anyone happy?
Let him sing songs of praise. Is any one of you sick?
He should call the elders of the church to pray over him
and anoint him with oil in the name of the Lord.
And the prayer offered in faith will make the sick person well;
the Lord will raise him up. If he has sinned, he will be forgiven.
JAMES 5:13-15, *NIV* (EMPHASIS ADDED)

When should we pray? Well, at one point in his letter to the Thessalonians, Paul tells us that we should pray without ceasing (see 1 Thess. 5:17), so I guess we should always have a prayer in our heart . . . however, there is one time in particular when we can pray . . . and that is . . . **When we are in trouble!**

This is the time when there isn't enough money to pay the bills.

When an earthquake destroys your home or business.

When your friend is acting like a jerk and destroying your friendship.

When your marriage is at a rough place.

When your child is hurting.

When you need help.

When you are confused.

When you are overwhelmed.

James urges us to open our mouth and pray in those times of trouble.

Recently, and during a period of just a few days, several things happened. I was working on a message that I would be giving that night at a GodChicks meeting and also working on a teaching that I would be giving the next weekend in church when a water pipe burst in our house and damaged the newly remodeled kitchen.

My kitchen was now filled with water as well as leak detection specialists and electricians. The damage was extensive enough that the carpet and some cabinets would have to be replaced. So, of course, all of those people needed to be organized. Philip was going out of town for a few days to a conference, which meant I was probably going to have to manage the repair process (Hey . . . trying to work on a message here!!). Then someone who should know better said some very mean and stupid things to me. My daughter, Paris, was not feeling well, and so she needed Mommy. The cute puppy that Philip got me cried all night, so no one got any sleep. In a planning meeting for our GodChicks conference, which was a few months away, I was feeling the weight of making sure we got it right . . . and then the diamond fell out of my wedding ring and was nowhere to be found; and then the power went out in my house right when I was finishing up the message for Sunday . . . ugh!!!

Just a bit of trouble!

And I found that complaining about any of it accomplished absolutely nothing! It never does.

So all I could do was take all of it to God in prayer!!

Trouble is part of life; but in the midst of it we have a choice. We can allow God to use it to mold us into the person He wants us to be, or we can allow it to destroy. The apostle James reminds us that we can choose the outcome of our troubles by opening our mouth and praying.

What kind of trouble are you in?

Is it financial?

Is it your marriage?

Is it a friendship?

Is there trouble at work?

There is no trouble too big or too small for our God. Or perhaps it's not happening to you but to someone else. Is someone in your world in trouble? Pray. Open your mouth and pray.

Steps to Awaken

• •

Rather than complain about any trouble you might be experiencing today, pray. Take a few minutes and pray right now. Pray that God would give you the strength to get through it, or deliver you from it.

Day 13

Is any one of you in trouble? He should pray. Is anyone happy?
Let him sing songs of praise. *Is any one of you sick? He should call
the elders of the church to pray over him and anoint him with
oil in the name of the Lord. And the prayer offered in faith will
make the sick person well; the Lord will raise him up.
If he has sinned, he will be forgiven.*
JAMES 5:13-15, *NIV* (EMPHASIS ADDED)

Gracias.
  Merci.
  Dank u.
  Вы(for my Russian princess Vera!).
  Grazie.
  Obrigado.
  σας ευχαριστούμε (for my Greek friend Christine!).

One of the first lessons in manners that we teach our children
is to say "thank you" when they receive something from someone, or when someone does something for them.

Recently, I reminded my daughter, as she was receiving gradu-
ation gifts, that writing and mailing thank-you notes to the
people who sent them was required.

Whether it is a delicious dinner, a birthday gift or a pulled-out
chair to help you get seated, saying "thank you" acknowledges
that the person did not have to do what they did, but you are
grateful that they did. Saying "thank you" is simply good manners and reveals a grateful heart.

In James 5:13, we are reminded that those who are happy, those
of us who have just been given a gift, those of us who are hav-

ing a great day, those of us who are on the mountaintop, must not forget who gave it to us.

Yes, God wants to hear from us when we are in trouble, but He also wants us to acknowledge His blessing when He has provided it.

In my life there have been so many reasons to say thank you! I have experienced God's healing power. I have found a sense of purpose for my life. I have a family who loves God and is committed to making the world a better place. I have enough food to eat. I have a roof over my head. I have a husband who loves me. And the list goes on and on.

Actually, the verse says to "sing songs of praise." Most people don't want me to sing my thank-yous to them. They are happy with the spoken version. ☺

In many churches, people sing songs of praise and worship to God. As we are singing those songs, it is the perfect time to remind ourselves of what God has done for us, and the many reasons we have to be grateful. So go ahead and sing!

Steps to Awaken

Read Romans 1:20-27. The last verses describe someone who is now far from God, but they didn't start that way. Their first step toward deception was a lack of gratitude. So let's make sure we don't start down that road! Make a list of what you are thankful for, and thank God today. (Feel free to sing it if you want!)

Day 14

*Are any of you suffering hardships? You should pray. Are any
of you happy? You should sing praises.* Are any of you sick?
You should call for the elders of the church to come
and pray over you, anointing you with oil in the name
of the Lord. Such a prayer offered in faith will heal
the sick, and the Lord will make you well. *And if you
have committed any sins, you will be forgiven.*
JAMES 5:13-15, *NLT* (EMPHASIS ADDED)

I hate being sick. I hate feeling bad, and I hate feeling weak. Often, my first response when I start to feel sick is to ask a doctor what to do, or Google my symptoms or go to bed. None of those actions are bad, and they may or may not need to be done; but really, our first response to any sickness should be prayer.

Go ahead with whatever treatment might be required, but ask for prayer first.

A few months ago, I was talking to a young mom who was dealing with her sick toddler. He had been throwing up, and was feverish. She was exhausted after days of this. Understandably. Finally, she called someone and said, "Let's pray." It was then that she got the strength necessary and her son got relief.

There were days during my cancer treatment when I had such strength—more strength than made sense in the natural. I would imagine it was because I had friends all over who were praying for me.

Sadly, there are so many people I know who are dealing with sickness—from morning sickness to cancer. So today, in my prayer time, I decided to pray for them—for all those I know who are not well. I opened my mouth and prayed for them. For peace, strength, healing and miracles.

> Let us then approach the throne of grace with confidence, so that we may receive mercy and find grace to help us in our time of need (Heb. 4:16, *NIV*).

Our boldness in approaching God comes from knowing that we are His beloved daughters. We have His permission! Maybe you could never really talk to your earthly dad. Maybe you feel like you have to walk on eggshells when you're with him—that you never know who you are going to get when you are with your dad. But with God, He is always the same. He is always full of mercy and grace, and He always listens.

And there is an element of boldness that comes when I know what the Bible has to say about a particular issue that I may be talking to God about.

I can confidently pray for those who are sick, because I know that God's will is healing.

> Praise the LORD, O my soul, and forget not all his benefits—who forgives all your sins *and heals all your diseases* (Ps. 103:2-3, *NIV*, emphasis added).

> He himself bore our sins in his body on the tree, so that we might die to sins and live for righteousness; *by his wounds you have been healed* (1 Pet. 2:24, *NIV*, emphasis added).

Steps to Awaken

Pray for someone in your world who is sick. Use one of the Scriptures above, or find another one in the Bible and pray that verse over her (or his) life.

Day 15

She opens her mouth in skillful and godly Wisdom, and on her tongue is the law of kindness [giving counsel and instruction].
PROVERBS 31:26, AMP

You and I should be capable of opening our mouths . . . not only with wisdom, but also with *godly* wisdom. We should be capable of giving the divine perspective to a situation . . . not just offering an opinion . . . but rather offering wisdom to overcome life's challenges.

Not long ago, I boarded a plane with my boarding pass in hand. As I approached my assigned seat, someone was sitting in it. I mentioned to the gentleman that he was in my seat, to which he replied, "I know, but I would really like to do some work with my colleague who is sitting here, so can you take my seat?"

He handed me his boarding pass and I headed to my new seat. When I got there, a woman was sitting in it.

I said, "Excuse me, but I think this is my seat."

She said, "Yes it is, but is it okay if you switch with me so that I can sit next to my daughter?"

"Sure."

I now proceeded to my new seat, only to find someone in it. *You are kidding me!!*

She asked if we could switch because she wanted to catch up with a friend.

Once again I agreed, and for the fourth time, I headed to a new seat.

This one was empty, so I quickly sat down. I smiled at the man sitting next to me, pulled out a book and began reading. In "international plane language," pulling out a book means "I don't want to talk."

However, the man next to me must not have understood "plane language," because he turned to me and said, "What do you do?"

I never exactly know how to respond to this question . . . because I think, *Which part of the day are you talking about?* I do a lot of things . . . I am wife, mother, pastor, author, speaker . . . and the list goes on. (Probably like yours!)

In response to him, I said, "Pastor." To which he quickly replied with great enthusiasm, "I have been *wanting* to talk to a pastor!!"

Now I got nervous.

Was he going to ask me to thoroughly break down the book of Leviticus? Or was he going to want me to discuss the pre-tribulation, post-tribulation arguments?

Nope.

None of that.

He said, "My wife and I just found out we are pregnant with triplets, and our marriage is already a little unstable. Do you have any suggestions on how to build a strong marriage?"

At first I was just silent, quietly asking God to forgive me for not realizing that He would not have moved me FOUR times if He did not have a plan in mind.

I have managed to stay married to the same man for 25 years, and we did just write a book about relationships and marriage, so I do have a few bits of marriage wisdom to share!

I opened my mouth, to the best of my ability, "in skillful and godly wisdom." I think the gentleman was encouraged and eventually left with some practical things he could do to strengthen his marriage.

Wisdom can be described as making the best use of knowledge, experience and understanding, and according to Proverbs 5:1, it has been learned by actual and costly experience.

So let's be those women who are willing to open our mouths with wisdom.

Not opinion, but wisdom.

Our opinion doesn't necessarily help anyone overcome life's challenges . . . godly wisdom does.

Steps to Awaken

Read Proverbs 5:1. Are your ears attentive today to hearing wisdom?

Day 16

For if you keep silent at this time, relief and deliverance shall arise for the Jews from elsewhere, but you and your father's house will perish.
ESTHER 4:14, *AMP*

Sometimes it is tricky to know when to keep silent and when to open your mouth.

After Mordecai's challenge to Esther in chapter 4, she knew she needed to open her mouth on behalf of her people. Their very lives depended on it.

What I found interesting in this story was that Esther had two opportunities to open her mouth, and she did not. She waited until the third time. I am not sure why. But there must have been something about the timing.

And let me just say, when opening your mouth . . . *timing is key!*

Queen Esther knew when to talk, and it wasn't the first time she was given an opportunity

If it is wisdom, it can wait for the right time.

I learned this the hard way.

A few years ago, I was sitting between Philip and our church administrator in a courtroom where we were waiting our turn to hear from the judge about some property issues. I knew the process could take awhile, so I brought a book to keep myself occupied. The other two did not, and so they began to talk. The judge looked back at us, pointed at me and said, "Woman, I told everyone that I expect quiet in this courtroom, so be quiet!"

I hadn't even been the one talking! (This is a first.)

I frowned at the other two for getting me in trouble. Soon, I noticed a woman coming into the courtroom and approaching the desk of the judge's assistant. She was given some papers to fill out and told to sit down. I could tell that she did not know what to do, because she did not speak English. She happened to sit on the bench in front of us. Perfect.

I could help her, because not only had I already filled out those papers, but I also speak Spanish and could explain it to her. I leaned forward and in Spanish began showing her what to do. I was feeling very good that I was helping her.

The judge did not see it that way.

"Woman, I told you to be quiet. Leave my courtroom!"

I was kicked out and had to go wait in the hall. Philip was trying hard not to laugh!

Good news is that the woman was kicked out too, so I could help her as we were both banished to the hallway.

So, opening your mouth with wisdom is good. And knowing the time to do it is even better!!

Steps to Awaken

Today make sure it is the right time as you share the wisdom that God has entrusted to you. Ask Him to help you know the time.

Day 17

And who knows but that you have come to
royal position for such a time as this?
ESTHER 4:14, *NIV*

I love the thought of time machines! (I know . . . I'm a little weird. ☺) I have been fascinated by the idea of time travel ever since I was a little girl. At one time, I even wanted to be an astronaut because I figured it would take a rocket to break through time travel! Even today, I love science fiction movies and time travel books.

I have visited different places in Europe and walked around some of the most beautiful ancient cities. There have been so many times when I wished I could stand on a busy street corner in Glasgow or London and twitch my little nose to travel back in time hundreds of years and see firsthand how people navigated life. (I wouldn't want to stay very long, because the no bathroom thing would really bother me.) For just a few minutes though, I would love to go back in time.

My fascination with history is not a bad thing. And yet, if I were always focused on *another* time, I am not sure I would be much use in *this* one. It is for *this* moment, *this* season, *this* time in history that you and I have been born.

Yes, we turn on the news and witness great devastation happening around the world. There have probably never been more wars, more pain and more agony.

But how awesome that God trusts you and me with this moment! He must think we can handle it! He must believe that you and I can bring solution to a very broken, very hurting world!

Esther was a young orphan turned queen. As a newly crowned queen, I wonder if she had moments when she thought she had it made—a real fairy tale ending to a rough beginning. Perhaps she imagined the rest of her life would be smooth sailing.

That is, until she heard about a plot to destroy her people.

It was then that she realized she was born "for such a time as this."

Unsummoned, she approached the king on behalf of her people. She risked her life, and in the end, she brought salvation to a whole nation.

We, too, have been born for such a time as this. The past is gone, and the future is not yet here. The only time we have to live is in the present. It is in our present that you and I can awaken to the needs of others, and like Queen Esther, bring salvation to those in need around us.

Steps to Awaken

Read or read again the book of Esther. Do you think you are here on the planet, at this time in history, for "such a time as this"? Or are you secretly longing for another time?

Day 18

A large crowd followed and pressed around him. And a woman was there who had been subject to bleeding for twelve years. She had suffered a great deal under the care of many doctors and had spent all she had, yet instead of getting better she grew worse. When she heard about Jesus, she came up behind him in the crowd and touched his cloak, because she thought, "If I just touch his clothes, I will be healed." Immediately her bleeding stopped and she felt in her body that she was freed from her suffering. At once Jesus realized that power had gone out from him. He turned around in the crowd and asked, "Who touched my clothes?" "You see the people crowding against you," his disciples answered, "and yet you can ask, 'Who touched me?'" But Jesus kept looking around to see who had done it. Then the woman, knowing what had happened to her, came and fell at his feet and, trembling with fear, told him the whole truth. He said to her, "Daughter, your faith has healed you. Go in peace and be freed from your suffering."

MARK 5:24-34, *NIV*

This story is told in the Gospels of Matthew, Luke and here in Mark, and it brings us face to face with a story of God's amazing healing power.

We get the picture of a very large group of people crowding around Jesus and His disciples. It must have been chaos! All sorts of people, from all over, bumping into Jesus.

It is interesting that only one touch caused Jesus to turn around. One touch brought healing. Why? I am not sure, but maybe the reason only one person received a miracle is because maybe only one person was expecting it.

Isn't that like some of us at times? Maybe we walk into church, sing a few songs and pray, and yet we leave unchanged. Jesus did say that where two or three were gathered in His name, He would be there in their midst (see Matt. 18:20). Yet we often only "bump into Him," not really believing that He wants to heal our hearts and our bodies.

Everybody has things they are dealing with.

For this woman, it was a physical illness.

For others, it might be a financial issue. Maybe you are feeling overwhelmed with debt and bills.

For some, it might be issues with family or friends. Maybe you are heartbroken over the divisions in your family.

For some, it might be addictions. Maybe you have some habits and patterns of behavior that have kept you bound.

For some, it might be fear or depression.

We all have our stuff.

And, like this woman, there really is only one place to get healing. There is only one place to get freedom.

At the feet of Jesus.

This story ends with Jesus calling the woman "daughter." This is the only place in the Scriptures where Jesus calls someone daughter.

Because of her disease, according to Jewish law, she had been considered unclean. Basically, for years she had lived as an outcast.

But now, not only was she healed in her body, but Jesus also called her "daughter." He was placing value on her.

He does the same for you and me. As we press through the busyness, pain and, sometimes, chaos of our lives and reach for Jesus, we will encounter healing and acceptance. We will leave any encounter with Him knowing that we are loved and valued.

We are not outcasts . . . regardless of our past.

Steps to Awaken

What issues in your life do you need to take to Jesus? Are you ready to believe that He wants to bring healing to that area?

Day 19

But if we confess our sins to him, he is faithful and just to forgive us our sins and to cleanse us from all wickedness.
1 JOHN 1:9, *NLT*

We all do stupid things. I know I do.

I choke on my own spit.

I trip over my own feet.

I have sent out twitters I probably shouldn't have.

A couple years ago I was teaching at our GodChicks Conference, and I was wearing a cute shirt with a different kind of neckline—the kind that you don't wear a normal bra under. I wore a strapless bra and didn't think much of it.

After the message, we ended the night with a party outside. (We're girls—we throw parties!) I was at the party, saying hi to friends and meeting new people, when I looked down and realized I had four LUMPS! That's right; my bra had completely slipped down to my stomach!

Somewhere, in some God-breathed moment of the message, my bra slipped right off!

(It took me months before I worked up the courage to watch the DVD of that teaching. It happened in a moment when I raised my hand! That DVD won't be for sale. ☺)

And yet, God is entrusting the salvation of the planet to people like you and me! . . . People who have been known to do some pretty stupid stuff!

We've all done dumb, embarrassing things.

And we've all done things we wish we hadn't. Things that aren't just silly or embarrassing but things that have caused us pain, or brought pain to others.

We've said things we wish we could take back. We've spent money on things we wish we had never purchased. We dated a guy we had no business dating. We made major decisions without listening to wisdom or reason.

We can't allow our mistakes to disqualify us from God's call in our lives. Honestly, sometimes we are our own worst enemy. We allow ourselves to be weighed down by guilt and then wonder why we aren't living light and free. Obviously, we can't pretend that we didn't do the thing we did . . . but there comes a time when we must move past it.

God doesn't hold our mistakes against us. In fact, He is quick to forgive! When we confess our sin to Jesus, the Bible says He is faithful and just . . . He forgives us! He sets us right back on course to fulfill His purposes for our life!

Aren't you glad we serve a forgiving God? Every day we get to experience His love, regardless of our shortcomings! Now that is something to smile about!

Steps to Awaken

Ask God to forgive you of a sin or mistake you have recently made. Thank God for His forgiveness, and commit to living today guilt-free and focused on fulfilling His purposes for your life!

Day 20

I have learned how to be content with whatever I have.
I know how to live on almost nothing or with everything.
I have learned the secret of living in every situation, whether it is
with a full stomach or empty, with plenty or little. For I can do
everything through Christ, who gives me strength.
PHILIPPIANS 4:11-13, *NLT*

Viktor Frankl was a successful neurologist and psychiatrist living in Austria with his wife before World War II began. On September 25, 1942, his life dramatically changed when he and his family were deported to the Theresienstadt concentration camp.

Over the next two years and eight months . . .
 . . . he was brutalized.
 . . . he was tortured.
 . . . he was faced with death daily.
 His parents and his wife were eventually murdered.

And yet, during the darkest years of his life in concentration camps, Dr. Frankl worked not only as a slave laborer, but also as a therapist for others imprisoned. He created programs to bring hope to fellow prisoners. He prolonged and saved the lives of countless Holocaust survivors before his liberation in 1945.

In his world-famous book recounting his experiences, *Man's Search for Meaning*, Dr. Frankl wrote, "Everything can be taken from a man or a woman but one thing: the last of human freedoms—to choose one's attitude in any given set of circumstances, to choose one's own way."[1]

Trials and unexpected challenges come to us all, and many without our choosing.

The betrayal of a close friend.
The loss of a job and financial security.
The doctor's diagnosis of cancer.
The lingering pain of a childhood drama.

We don't always get to choose our battles, but we do get to choose our attitude. The way we manage our emotions and what we choose to focus on determine what type of strength we awaken to each day. When we meditate on God's Word, our attitude changes for the better! We become women of strength, ready to face our challenges head-on! We get to experience peace and joy, confident that we can do all things through Christ who gives us strength!

Steps to Awaken

Write down the facts of a current challenge you are facing. Balance that with what the truth of God's Word says about it. As you read and think about God's Word, pray that God will help you make changes to your current attitude.

Note
1. Viktor Frankl, *Man's Search for Meaning* (Boston: Beacon Press, 2006).

Day 21

Arise, shine, for your light has come, and the glory of the LORD rises upon you. See, darkness covers the earth and thick darkness is over the peoples, but the LORD rises upon you and his glory appears over you.
ISAIAH 60:1-2, *NIV*

Have you ever found yourself standing in a dark season of life, knee-deep in what felt like unearthed ground and the remains of rubble?

I have.

I remember the beginning of our marriage, when I was ready to pack my bags and walk out the door. We thought we were too different from each other, and I was convinced I had married the wrong guy . . . dark moment.

I remember standing before our church family, on Super Bowl Sunday in 2005, to tell them I had been diagnosed with breast cancer. The next morning, when the reality hit, I wasn't sure I'd be able to get out of bed . . . very dark moment.

I remember countless moments standing in Uganda, Guatemala, Peru and some of the poorest places on the planet, wondering how God would restore, repair and rebuild the cities . . . and the people . . . dark moments that made my dark moments look suddenly lighter.

"See, darkness covers the earth and thick darkness is over the peoples." Isaiah, as an ambassador for God, recognized that the nation was living in a dark time. Economic crisis, war, addictions, diseases plagued the people. As King Solomon tells us in Ecclesiastes 1:9, "there is nothing new under the sun" (*NIV*).

The battles haven't changed much throughout the ages, but with each new generation, we have to engage in this war against injustice.

Isaiah 60 speaks of restoration. God's plan was to rebuild the city through His people whom He had rescued from exile and slavery so they would be a light to other nations—His light illuminating every dark place through them. ARISE . . . SHINE . . . for your light has come, and the glory of the LORD rises upon you.

In essence, he's encouraging them by saying (without much sympathy, I notice!!): I know it's a dark time; I know that everywhere you turn you see a scary situation; I know that everywhere you look there is poverty, disease, hurting people, brokenness; but come on, rise up—we've got a war to fight, and God's glory will light the way.

The word "glory" comes from the Greek word *doxa*, which means "dignity."[1] Dignity speaks to our value—it means worthy of esteem or respect. It's almost like Isaiah is saying, "I know you were exiles and slaves in your past, and I know you came home to a very messy city; but dignity appears over you and you are worthy—because God is and says you are—of esteem and respect." In other words, you have a right . . . perhaps an obligation to shine in the midst of dark times.

That was a dark time in my marriage, but I had an obligation—to my future children, to the church we were building together, to the destiny God had prepared for me—to rise in that darkness, to respect and connect with Philip to overcome our challenges (26 years later, we just . . . or finally finished our first book together!). A cancer diagnosis was a dark time for our family, but I had to rise in adversity and proclaim God's ability to heal and deliver me (five years later, still cancer free!).

In the darkest corners of the world, God is using His people to shine a light. His glory has risen in us and we have risen in Him to answer the call to reach a lost and broken world.

Make the choice to rise in your dark season. Make the choice to rise in a dark world. Our God has granted you dignity, worth, value . . . so rise up in His name.

Steps to Awaken

Find someone in your world who could use a little light. Find a mom with a newborn and make dinner for her. Bring a latte to a co-worker (try the one you really can't stand). Call your mentor and say thank you . . . find a way to shine.

Note

1. James Strong, *Strong's Exhaustive Concordance of the Bible*, "doxa," Greek word #1391. http://strongsnumbers.com/greek/1391.htm.

Day 22

For you were once darkness, but now you are light in the Lord.
Live as children of light (for the fruit of the light consists in all goodness,
righteousness and truth) and find out what pleases the Lord.
EPHESIANS 5:8-10, *NIV* (EMPHASIS ADDED)

As a little girl, I remember sitting on my daddy's lap. I remember feeling safe and feeling loved. I knew that I could tell him, without hesitation, about my hurts, needs and wants, and he would do his best to take care of them.

"Daddy, can I have this? Daddy, I need that." Not sure I really needed all that I asked for . . . but without question, I relied on my father to take care of me.

And he did . . . because he loves me, his daughter.

Maybe you did not have a dad whose lap you could sit on. Maybe he was not around, or maybe you were neglected or abused and can't even relate to the picture I've painted. I am so sorry. Would you be willing to let God love you like the perfect Father He is? He will never neglect or abuse you.

Our heavenly Father loves us perfectly. When we are in need, we can approach Him, confident that He will take care of us. We can "sit on His lap" and let Him know exactly what we need.

"Heavenly Father, this is my hurt. This is my pain." We can trust Him to heal and mend our hearts.

"Heavenly Father, this is what I need." We can rely on Him to provide for us.

Why? Because we are His loved-beyond-measure daughters.

And yet, all little daughters grow up to be women. We still trust in and rely on our fathers' care; but as we mature, we begin to talk differently to our fathers. We seek not only *to be taken care of*, but also *to care of* our fathers. Occasionally, I still sit on my dad's lap, but mainly it is to love on him and to ask what I can do for him.

In the same way, as we begin to mature in our faith, we seek not only to receive from God, but also to bless Him.

We see ourselves not only as young daughters, but also as maturing women.

As women, we approach our heavenly Father and ask, "What can I do for *You* today? How can I care for the things *You* care about today?"

When we begin to pray like this, God shows us how we can be used by Him in our everyday lives to make a great difference in the world today. We begin to realize the great role God has purposed for His women at this time in history!

Steps to Awaken

Ask your heavenly Father, "What can I do for You today? Is there a person You need me to talk to? Is there someone I need to give something to?"

Day 23

*Hear now this, O foolish people without understanding
or heart, who have eyes and see not.*
JEREMIAH 5:21, *AMP*

Sometimes we can go through life on autopilot, not really seeing what is in front of us.

Have you ever arrived home from work, and wondered how you got there??? Because you don't remember anything about your drive home!!

If we are going to shine our light . . . to live open and generous lives . . . we can't go through life like that! Our "eyes" have to be open!

Here are some actual labels of instruction on consumer goods . . . these labels are pretty amazing. I don't know if it's because we have so many lawsuits in our country or because people write letters of complaint, or what. But is anyone actually seeing these labels??

On the instructions for a hair dryer it said, "Don't use while sleeping." I am just wondering if someone tried this. Sometimes Philip might say to me in the morning, "Holly, you snored, you tossed and turned"; but I have never heard him say, "There you were, styling your hair again while you were asleep!"

On the instructions that came with an iron it said, "Do not iron clothes while on your body." Really??? I smell a lawsuit with that one! If you are in that much of a hurry, go with wrinkles!

On a Swedish chainsaw it says, "Don't attempt to stop blade with hands." I can't even imagine that one!

On a tube of Preparation H . . . "Do not take orally." I can only imagine the letter someone must have written . . . "Dear Preparation H, I ate the whole tube, and I still have hemorrhoids."

Okay, I am kind of playing here, but the truth is that we go through many of our days not seeing what might be right in front of us.

The Gospel of Luke, chapter 10, tells us the story of the Good Samaritan. A man was wounded by the side of a road, and when two religious people saw him, they looked at him and walked on by. Then the Samaritan man came to where the wounded man was, and he SAW . . . two others had passed by and looked . . . but truly seeing a situation leads to action. The Samaritan saw the wounded man and was moved with pity and sympathy, and so he did something.

Every day situations come across our path, and if our eyes are open and we are not just on autopilot, we can see that we are being given a chance to be the hand of God.

So let's keep our eyes open . . . because often the reason we are being given a chance to see is so that we can be a part of the solution.

Steps to Awaken

When you are walking or driving around today, do your best to really see your world. Do you see the people? Do you see a situation you could help with?

Day 24

Open my eyes so I can see what you show me
of your miracle-wonders.
PSALM 119:18, *THE MESSAGE*

Usually one of the first things we do after we wake up in the morning is open our eyes. We might lie there in bed and look around for a minute, wishing we could close our eyes again! Or we might jump right up. But our day starts when our eyes are open; or as it sometimes goes with me . . . barely open until I get some coffee!

The opening of our eyes in this Scripture is not just the biological process of lifting our lids, but of opening our heart.
Opening our heart to wonder.
Opening our heart to the possibilities.

A few years ago at our annual GodChicks conference in Los Angeles, I wanted to create a moment that would take the women's breath away—one of those moments when they would say, "Ahh!" I am just not sure we have enough of those moments . . .

After the Friday evening session, the women walked out to the courtyard to enjoy the after-party. What they encountered as they arrived was a giraffe. Yep. A real-live giraffe. Right in the middle of the city. He was adorable as he bent down and batted his eyelashes. Hundreds of women stood around laughing and taking photos. It was one of those take-your-breath-away wondrous moments, and I just loved it. There was no particular reason to have a giraffe; I just wanted to create a moment.

In the book of Numbers, chapter 13, God tells Moses that He is giving the Promised Land to the children of Israel. He tells

Moses to send out 12 men to explore what will soon become their new home.

Ten of those men came back and spoke of the big giants and the fortified cities. They saw the problem.

Joshua and Caleb, 2 of the 12 spies, saw the same land. They saw the richness of the land, with all its big fruit and big cities. They saw the giants; they just did not see them as a problem. Maybe they figured that the giants had merely been guarding the abundance of the land for the Israelites for all these years.

It's all about how you see a situation.

Sadly, the negative report of the 10 outweighed the positive report of the 2. And God was very angry. He actually wanted to disinherit all the people and start over with Moses. But Moses talked Him out of it. It really is a great story.

Seeing the negative, seeing what can't be done, is never pleasing to God.

How many times have we interpreted what we see like that?

For many of us, perhaps God has done something awesome.
    Healed our body.
    Brought peace to our heart.
    Reconciled a relationship.
    And yet . . . we can get to a point where we forget . . . where we have stopped seeing the wondrous things.

Maybe it's our marriage.
    Do you see the challenge you are facing as one more piece of evidence for hopelessness, or do you choose to see it as a step on the way to a great marriage?

Maybe it's our job.

Remember when you first got that job? You were so excited! This was an answer to prayer. God gave you this job, and now you can barely get out of bed to get there. Maybe somewhere along the way you stopped seeing the purpose and the possibilities.

Maybe it's with each other.

If you look for fault in someone, you will find it. It's not that difficult.

If we look for mistakes, we will find them.

But how about if we look for the wondrous things, the great things in each other?

Steps to Awaken

• •

Today, find three wondrous things that are in your world. Some of these things might have been right in front of you for years!

Day 25

Above all else, you must live in a way that brings honor
to the good news about Christ. *Then, whether I visit you or not,
I will hear that all of you think alike. I will know that you
are working together and that you are struggling side by side
to get others to believe the good news.*
PHILIPPIANS 1:27, *CEV* (EMPHASIS ADDED)

In recent years, we have seen the rise of the X-Games—extreme
stunts with skateboards and bicycles and skis. I saw a TV show
that featured street luging—an underground sport in which
people race downhill on a handmade luge through city streets
and reach speeds over 90 miles per hour. Now why would anyone do that????

I'm not sure that I would ever participate in "extreme sports."
However, I do believe that God is calling us to live an extreme
life.

ex·treme /[*ik-streem*]: farthest removed from the ordinary or average.[1]

Perhaps if the apostle Paul were here today, he might word his
comments to the Philippians this way, "Above all else you must
LIVE EXTREME (you must exceed the usual, ordinary and the
average—in your church, home, work, walk and purity) . . . so
that people will be so blown away by how you live, that they will
believe the good news and turn to God."

Yep . . . that's the kind of life I want to live . . . the farthest removed from ordinary or average! Being extreme is being extravagant and uncompromising. We are called to be extremely
faithful, extremely capable, extremely generous, extremely loving, extremely determined.

God went to the extreme for our sake. God, Creator of the universe, the King of kings and the Lord of lords, stripped Himself of His royal position in heaven and came to earth as a man, as Jesus. But He didn't stop there; He fiercely pursued and carried out His mission to redeem mankind and, as the apostle Paul so brilliantly wrote, He "carried His obedience to the extreme of death, even to the death of the cross!" (Phil. 2:8, *AMP*).

Rarely am I speechless, but this thought, this kind of love, this extreme generosity almost renders me without words.

Extreme Life.

We are called, and chosen, to live an extreme life in God.

Steps to Awaken

Think about the extreme life that Jesus lived for us. Think about the extravagant and uncompromising choice He made to save us. Is there a way you can be extreme today?

Note

1. Dictionary.com (New York: Random House, Inc., 2010), s.v. "extreme." http://dictionary.reference.com/browse/extreme.

Day 26

If we are faithless [do not believe and are untrue to Him],
He remains true (faithful to His Word and His righteous character),
for He cannot deny Himself.
2 TIMOTHY 2:13, *AMP*

One of the ways we can choose to be extreme is in our faithfulness. This is often opposite of what we see daily through our media, in our schools, in our churches and even in our own homes.

Many people say that close to 50 percent of marriages end in divorce.

Seven thousand high school students drop out of school every day in the USA, and only about 70 percent of students graduate.[1]

Also in America, it is estimated that 3,500 to 4,000 churches close their doors every year.[2]

A recent study in the UK says that the average family spends less than one hour a day together.[3]

We struggle with faithfulness in almost every area of our lives.

The ability to remain faithful is a mark of good character. As Paul told Timothy (and us) in the Scripture above, faithfulness is God's character. Even when we are not faithful to God, He remains faithful to us.

Here's what I've noticed: It's easy to be faithful when it's not costing us anything. But "extreme" is revealed in a challenging moment. Sitting on a surfboard in still water is not extreme; it becomes extreme when there is a 20-foot wave to navigate.

It is easy to be faithful when work is going along the way you want it to, when you are getting what you want out of it. But what about when the moment requires going beyond ordinary? Can you remain faithful then?

Our marriage had better be extreme, because average marriages are failing at an alarming rate. We must go beyond average.

It is easy to be faithful in your marriage when it is going great— when he is giving you everything you need. But what about when it costs you?

There are some moments in a marriage when we get the opportunity to prove our extreme faithfulness. When those "lovin' feelings" just aren't there.

Those moments can come in the first year or two, when you realize that marriage is hard and you can't always get your way. Or maybe in year seven or eight, when you might have toddlers running around; you are feeling drained and you can't seem to connect with your husband. Or possibly in year 25, when the kids leave home, and you don't really know the man you married.
Faithfulness is proved in those times.

We must be extreme in our faithfulness to God. Through the years, I have met people who seemed to have a relationship with God. They worshiped and read their Bible. And then they encountered a hard time . . . got divorced . . . lost a job . . . experienced the death of a loved one . . . and they walked away from God. They couldn't remain faithful in the hard times. They lost faith in the times when there seemed to be no answer.

Let's not be people who quit when our faithfulness costs us something.

So many people do.

But you and I are not most people—we are God's people, and we must determine to be extreme in our faithfulness. Let's continue to do what's right, even when we don't feel like it.

Steps to Awaken

In what area is your faithfulness waning the most? Do the hard thing, the right thing . . . even though you don't feel like it.

Notes

1. "High School Dropout Crisis Threatens U.S. Economic Growth and Competitiveness, Witnesses Tell House Panel," Committee on Education and Labor, May 12, 2009. http://edlabor.house.gov/newsroom/2009/05/high-school-dropout-crisis-thr.shtml.
2. D. Goodmanson, "The Future Dying Church," Goodmanson.com. http://www.goodmanson.com/church/the-future-dying-church/.
3. "How Long Does the Average Family Spend Together Each Day? 49 Minutes," Woolley & Co. Solicitors, June 19, 2010. http://www.family-lawfirm.co.uk/News/June-2010/How-long-does-the-average-family-spend-together-each-day-49-minutes.aspx.

Day 27

A capable, intelligent, and virtuous woman—who is he
who can find her? She is far more precious than jewels and
her value is far above rubies or pearls.
PROVERBS 31:10, *AMP*

When I first read about the woman of Proverbs 31, I was a bit intimidated by her. She just seemed able to do everything. And not only do everything . . . but also at the end of the chapter . . . her family calls her "blessed."

Definitely capable.

"Capable" means to have the ability or capacity for. Perhaps it's her capabilities that overwhelmed me. Was there anything this woman couldn't do?!

However, as I began to study this chapter, I realized that in many ways her life was to be a kind of blueprint for yours and mine.

With God's help, we are to be extremely capable women.

Extremely capable—mentally, emotionally, physically and spiritually.

The journey to increasing external capacity is an internal wrestling. Until we increase on the inside, we will not increase on the outside.

Life does seem to hit us in spurts . . . you know what I mean.
You're running along in your lane when suddenly your boss decides to test your skills on a new project . . . only this is the week your daughter's science project is due . . . and she forgot to

start it. On top of that, your husband is driving you . . . well . . . insane. And the hot water heater has decided to burst, despite the fact that your emergency fund is nonexistent and you're not quite sure how the mortgage will get paid.

This is exactly the time to be extremely capable! Internally, it's time to rise up. When life hits us, it's time to roll up our sleeves and do the work. We are capable women who can accomplish the tasks in front of us if we commit to not letting the internal pressures of feeling incapable and overwhelmed take us over.

Sometimes we give up before we even start!

How many times have you collapsed in tears on the floor, on the couch . . . in front of the bathroom mirror, before you have even tried to tackle the increased tasks before you?

Proverbs 31:18 says, "She senses the worth of her work, is in no hurry to call it quits for the day" (*THE MESSAGE*). Sometimes when we are in the seemingly routine tasks of our day, we can lose sight of the worth of our work. And once we do that, we hold back and our capacity to handle our world shrinks.

You have the ability, in God, to manage all that is in your life! Don't pull back.

Don't quit before you start! Being extremely capable starts with a decision. Decide to rise. God is your provider, your healer, your very present help in time of need. Remember, you are His daughter. You can do it!!

Steps to Awaken

Make a list of the tasks you have to accomplish today. Come up with a realistic plan to accomplish them. Make a decision to rise . . . and then go for it!

Day 28

Truly I tell you, whoever says to this mountain, Be lifted up and thrown into the sea! and does not doubt at all in his heart but believes that what he says will take place, it will be done for him. For this reason I am telling you, whatever you ask for in prayer, believe (trust and be confident) that it is granted to you, and you will [get it].

MARK 11:23-24, *AMP*

This is an awesome promise, isn't it! It is underlined in most of my Bibles. Oh, and here is the rest of that portion of Scripture, which is NOT underlined:

And whenever you stand praying, if you have anything against anyone, forgive him and let it drop (leave it, let it go), in order that your Father Who is in heaven may also forgive you your [own] failings and short-comings and let them drop. But if you do not forgive, neither will your Father in heaven forgive your failings and shortcomings (Mark 11:25-26, *AMP*).

I am pretty sure that verse means just what it says: We are to practice extreme forgiveness.

As we go through life, we will have the opportunity to offend and to be offended. My strengths can offend you . . . my weaknesses . . . my personality . . . my issues . . . my failures. Lots of chances to be offended! In Luke 17, Jesus told us that we will have lots of opportunity to show forgiveness to others. So, basically, this means that it is impossible to live life and not have the opportunity to get offended.

And even if he sins against you seven times in a day, and turns to you seven times and says, I repent [I am sorry], you must forgive him (give up resentment and consider the offense as recalled and annulled) (Luke 17:4, *AMP*).

I never *feel* like forgiving anyone . . . not the first time, and certainly not the seventh or the seventieth! But if I want my sins to be forgiven, then extending forgiveness is my only option. Forgiveness is a decision, not a feeling. Often I need to forgive a person daily, until the thought no longer hurts my heart or makes me mad.

I am not suggesting that you must become best friends with the person who continues to betray you. But you do need to forgive him or her, whether you ever see the person again. Whether that person asks for forgiveness or not. Jesus forgave us long before we asked for it.

If we don't forgive, then we ourselves are trapped. Freedom comes through forgiveness.

I have a friend who has worked with the children in northern Uganda who were kidnapped and forced into being soldiers. Years later, these young people are free from their captors. But real freedom for them began when they forgave those who captured them. I can't imagine how hard it must have been for them to forgive those who killed their friends and forced them to kill their own families. It's shocking to believe that such brutality exists. And yet today, many of these young people have found joy again . . . and it began when they were able to forgive.

We must make the decision to not let the bitter root of unforgiveness take hold of our lives. Failure to make this decision will only bring destruction.

Steps to Awaken

You probably knew this was coming, so here it is! Who do you need to forgive? Whether that person is alive or has passed away, make the decision today to forgive him or her. And remember, it is a decision . . . not a feeling.

Day 29

My heart is stirred by a noble theme as I recite my verses for the king;
my tongue is the pen of a skillful writer.
PSALM 45:1, *NIV*

According to some statistics that I've read, the average person spends one-fifth of his or her life talking. In fact, if all of our words were put into print, the result would be this: The words from a single day would fill a 50-page book. In a year's time the average person's words would fill 132 books of 200 pages each!

As women, our daily words might make a 100-page book!
Wow!
That is a lot of words!

Your words are writing the story of your life.
"I love you."
"You're important to me."
"Thank you so much."
"How can I repay you?"
"You look really nice today."
"I'm proud of you."
"Will you marry me?"
"I hate you."
"You disgust me."
"I wish you had never been born."
"You make me sick."
"I want a divorce."
All of those words affect us—in a positive or a negative way.

Words are important. Words frame our world. Our hearts are stirred as we speak words of truth, of nobility, of wisdom . . . and if our tongues are to be the pens of a *skillful* writer, then we've got some work to do!

Whatever we speak out of our mouths is an indication of how we feel about ourselves on the inside. If we are critical, it has nothing to do with the people we criticize and everything to do with how we feel about ourselves. If we withhold compliments, perhaps it reveals jealousy lurking in our hearts.

On the other hand, if we are loving, gracious and forgiving, if we are kind with our words, the people in our world can see that we understand that we are loved, graced by God and forgiven. Our words reveal Christ's character on the inside of us.

What's coming out of your mouth? Do you encourage and affirm your husband as he is—or do you nag him and try to change him? By your words, do your children know they are loved—or do they have to assume what you mean through silence or sideways comments? Do our families, friends, co-workers, employees, bosses and anyone else in our sphere of influence know how much we value their contribution to our lives?

Our words also reveal Christ's purpose on the inside of us. Again, words frame our world . . . words speak value, declare the truth of God's Word, remind us and others of who we are. Your past does not have to dictate your future. Who you are right now can be transformed into the woman God has designed you to be. You have a destiny, a purpose, that no one else can fulfill. Begin to declare the truth over your life today—set the atmosphere of your life . . . and start with your words.

Steps to Awaken

Pay careful attention to the words you speak today. Choose them carefully.

Day 30

*Now listen, daughter, don't miss a word: forget your country,
put your home behind you. Be here—the king is wild for you.
Since he's your lord, adore him.*
PSALM 45:10-11, *THE MESSAGE*

Each of us has a past, a history, a story. We've had hurtful experiences. We've made poor choices, lived through some strenuous and perhaps heartbreaking circumstances and then have encountered the love of God.

When we encounter His love, we begin to read the Bible to learn who God is and who we are in Him. His Word holds transforming power that heals us, changes us and causes our future to line up with the truth of His Word rather than the lies of our past.

In this verse we are challenged to *be here*. And it is hard to be *here*, if we can't step beyond our past. It is so important to leave behind *what was* and to step into *what is*.

When we cling to our past, we bring unnecessary baggage into our present. We can bring attitudes and fears into current relationships, and then it is next to impossible to "be here," which is another way of saying to "be present." When we are focused on our past, we cannot enjoy what's present and are not ready for our future. And your future is bright . . . full of promise.

So, be here! The King is wild for you! The forgiving nature of our Savior releases us from our past. His blood on the cross washes us clean and makes ALL things new (see 2 Corinthians 5:17 and Revelation 21:5). You have been adopted into God's family—there is now a marriage between you and heaven. Forget your past; put it all behind you. Be here in your present relationship with Christ, who is wild for you.

He is wild for you.

God is not merely tolerating you.

He is not overlooking you.

His love for you is not casual.

He is wild for you!

This psalm is a song of love. There is nothing passive about it. You are loved.

And since we are so loved, since He is our Lord, our King, let's adore Him. Let's honor Him with our lives, worship Him with abandon and love Him like none other.

Steps to Awaken

Read the whole of Psalm 45. Which verse speaks to you the most?

Day 31

He said to the crowd: "When you see a cloud rising in the west, immediately you say, 'It's going to rain,' and it does. And when the south wind blows, you say, 'It's going to be hot,' and it is. Hypocrites! You know how to interpret the appearance of the earth and the sky. How is it that you don't know how to interpret this present time?

LUKE 12:54-56, *NIV*

In Southern California, we don't really get to experience the four seasons. Palm trees don't change colors, and I have yet to build a snowman in my front yard! Basically, we live in perpetual spring and summer. But do I love where I live!

However, those of you who live elsewhere are much better at preparing for changing seasons. You've learned to be alert to the indicators that a new season is coming. When winter approaches, you pull in the lawn furniture. You winterize (whatever the heck that is) your garden. You get the snow shovel and rake out from the basement.

You are alert to a coming season change.

Those who live in Florida and along the Atlantic coast are alert for hurricanes during the summer and fall months.

They recognize when it might be hurricane season.

I wonder what season of life you are in right now. Is it a season of growth and success? Is it a season full of difficult challenges? Is it a season of waiting and trusting in God's perfect timing and provision? Is it a season of transition and change?

Maybe you've just received a big promotion that is both exciting and a little scary. Maybe you are recently engaged and planning your wedding. Maybe you have just gotten a doctor's report you wish you hadn't. Maybe you are moving to a new city, far away from family and friends.

Jesus teaches us in Luke 12 to understand the season we are in.

He teaches us to be ALERT to the seasons in our life.

> **alert** [*uh-lurt*]: fully aware and attentive; *wide-awake*; keen.[1]

God is asking you and me to look at our current season of life with wide-awake eyes. Some seasons are shorter than others, but each season of life comes with its own responsibilities. If we are going to successfully navigate through whatever season we are in, we will need to see the relationships we must nurture, the needs we must meet, the decisions we must make, and the opportunities we must take to serve.

The great news is that we can pray for alert, wide-awake eyes in our current season! When we pray for God to open our eyes, He is faithful to do just that! He will give us the needed wisdom as well as show us how to prepare and navigate through whatever season we are in!

Steps to Awaken

Spend a few minutes praying to God, asking the Holy Spirit to show you practical ways you can prepare for and navigate through the season you are currently in. What character traits do you think you might need to help you get through this season?

Note

1. Dictionary.com (New York: Random House, Inc., 2010), s.v. "alert." http://diction ary.reference.com/browse/alert.

Day 32

You are all sons of the light and sons of the day.
We do not belong to the night or to the darkness. So then,
let us not be like others, who are asleep,
but let us be alert and self-controlled.
1 THESSALONIANS 5:5-6, *NIV* (EMPHASIS ADDED)

Like me, you have probably watched a few television cop shows and seen officers on a stakeout. The officers have to be alert and ready to catch the bad guy they are waiting for. They can't just sit around and play games or check their twitter accounts on their iPhones. But I am sure they are tempted to do so. In the long, dark hours of the night, while they wait, they are tempted to get momentarily distracted.

They must get a bit sleepy waiting for the culprit. After the third or fourth cup of coffee wears off, I am sure it gets harder and harder to stay awake.

Perhaps after a few hours the officers doubt that the criminal is going to show up.

And maybe they begin to reason with each other that sticking around isn't worth it. The comfort of their beds seems a hundred times better than the stuffy van they are waiting in. They debate whether or not to give up and call it a night.

What if they did leave? Or what if they did fall asleep?

They would miss the very assignment they were waiting there to accomplish.

Maybe you and I are on a stakeout of sorts . . .

I, Paul, am a devoted slave of Jesus Christ on assignment (Rom. 1:1, *THE MESSAGE*).

We all have an assignment from God. He has given each of us a plan and a purpose to fulfill. We can't get distracted or fall asleep. We have to be alert to what's around us. We have to stay vigilant.

If we don't, we might miss the very assignment God has for us.

If we are not alert, we could miss out on opportunities to really connect with our husband.

We could miss out on volunteering and contributing in our church.

We could miss out on an important moment with our kids.

We could miss out on noticing that our friend desperately needs to talk.

We could miss out on the life God intended for us to live.

Let's commit to be women who are alert and vigilant right where God has put us. Let's be aware of the various ways the enemy would try to get us distracted and worn out. Let's stay alert to recognize God's grace and love at work in our lives. And let's be mindful of the ways we can love God and the people around us more deeply.

Steps to Awaken

Are you distracted by something in your life that is keeping you from being fully alert? Spend a few minutes asking God to keep you alert to your assignment.

Day 33

Keep vigilant watch over your heart; that's where life starts.
PROVERBS 4:23, *THE MESSAGE*

After I was diagnosed with breast cancer, I spent a couple of weeks in a hospital. One of the tests administered was what is called a "stress test." I was hooked up to a machine that monitored different areas in my body. Before the test began, the doctor asked me a simple question.

"How much stress are you experiencing at this point in your life?"

I thought about it for a minute and then honestly replied, "I'm doing pretty good. I mean, I know I am battling cancer, but all things considered, I'm good."

The doctor simply said, "Okay."

After the test was completed and an analysis on my stress levels had been gathered, the doctor gave me the news.

"Holly," the doctor began, "just so you know, based on what is going on in your adrenal glands, the level of stress you are experiencing is as if you were staring a roaring lion in the face."
    A roaring lion???!!!
    Yikes!!!
    And I had been totally unaware.

Needless to say, I had a few changes to make. Once I was alert to what was taking place in my body, I had work to do if I was ever going to get healthy again! I had to learn to be aware of what stresses me, and then how to manage it. I researched and read dozens and dozens of books on health and stress. I prayed and asked the Holy Spirit for peace and wisdom. And I made some changes to the foods I eat, the exercise I do and the amount of rest I get.

The thing about my story is that if I hadn't been alerted to what was happening within me, I would have never known how to overcome the battle I was facing.

The same is true for you today. We are all facing different battles.

Battles at work, at home, with our finances, our health . . .

The key to winning these battles is becoming alert to the conditions of our hearts.

What is the condition of your heart today?
    Are you worried and overwhelmed?
    Are you discouraged and doubting?
    Are you heartbroken by past hurts?
    Are you growing frustrated and impatient?

Once you become alert to the present condition of your heart, you can make some necessary changes and, perhaps, get some help. And you can approach your heavenly Father with confidence and ask Him to lead you to a place of health and strength. You can trust that He will care for you and bring you hope and victory!

Steps to Awaken

Find a Bible verse that relates to the condition of your heart today or the current battle you are facing, and let the promise found in that verse encourage and strengthen your heart.

Day 34

Endure hardship with us like a good soldier of Christ Jesus.
2 TIMOTHY 2:3, *NIV*

en·dure [*en-door*]—*verb*—to hold out against; sustain without impairment or yielding; undergo.[1]

I've always been told, "Choose your battles." That is probably good advice in marriage and parenting. ☺

But there are some battles that I didn't choose to fight. They chose me.

I didn't choose to battle cancer. I just knew that if I was going to survive it, I was going to have to fight it. And fight it, I did!

Perhaps you are facing some battles not of your choosing.

We don't always get to choose our battles, but we do get to choose whether or not we will fight. And we do get to choose whether or not we will endure.

I have heard there are endurance races held around the world called *ultra-marathons*. These involve running longer than the traditional marathon and often have extreme course obstacles, elevation changes and rugged terrain. Sometimes they are even run in very bad weather. I have no desire to sign up for one of these endurance races! I am not sure I see the purpose in running longer than a traditional marathon!!

But I like the thought of being a person who can endure through distance, bad weather, pain, hills . . . and whatever obstacles come up. Sometimes in our very comfortable American life, we are not taught to endure, so we collapse at the first or second obstacle. Or we just can't make it through another day.

You and I need to be the kind of women who endure. Not bitter or just "tolerating" something, but rather enduring with strength and determination until we cross the finish line.

Like a good soldier, we must determine to awaken the warrior within us.

What battles are you facing today? What are you willing to fight for and endure until you see some sort of breakthrough?

Your marriage?
Your children?
Your friendships?
Your health?
Your finances?
Your joy? (Joy is an approach to life rather than a reaction to it. In every season of life, joy is something worth fighting for.)

Let's determine to be women who rise up and fight in the midst of the battles. Let's be committed to enduring hardships like good soldiers of Christ Jesus, and in doing so, experience the victorious life Jesus has for each of us!

Steps to Awaken

· ·

What battle are you facing? Write it down on a piece of paper, and underneath it explain how you will fight the battle you are currently facing.

Note
1. Dictionary.com (New York: Random House, Inc., 2010), s.v. "endure." http://dictionary.reference.com/browse/survive.

Day 35

*For all His ordinances were before me, and I put not away
His statutes from me. . . . As for God, His way is perfect!
The word of the Lord is tested and tried; He is a shield to all those
who take refuge and put their trust in Him.*

PSALM 18:22,30, AMP

I remember hearing about POWs in Vietnam who were tortured to extract classified information. One of the tools the enemy used was deception. The torturer would say, "Your country has forgotten all about you. You don't matter to them." If the enemy could get the captured soldier to believe that, then they could probably get the information they needed. It all started with a lie.

Defeat always starts with a lie.

As daughters of the King, we have an enemy. His greatest weapons are lies and deception. In fact, his *only* weapons are lies and deception.

But, we don't have to become a casualty of his war. When the enemy tries to bombard us with lies, we have faith in Jesus and the truth of His Word to protect and defend us.

The promises found in the Bible are written for you and me, not merely to read in our spare time or at church, but to wield as the ultimate weapon of defense (and offense) in battle. Not only is the Word of God our sword, but along with faith it is also our shield (see Eph. 6:16-17). It can shield us from whatever arrow the enemy would aim our way.

What lie is the enemy attempting to attack you with? What weakness is he preying on in your mind?

I don't have what it takes.

The Bible says in Philippians 4:13, "I can do everything through Him who gives me strength" (*NIV*).

I am not enough.

The Bible says in Psalm 139:14, "I praise you because I am fearfully and wonderfully made; your works are wonderful. I know that full well" (*NIV*).

I am all alone.

Jesus promises in Matthew 28:20, "And surely I am with you always, to the very end of the age" (*NIV*).

I deserve this sickness.

The Bible says in Luke 4:40, "The people brought to Jesus all who had various kinds of sickness, and laying his hands on each one, he healed them" (*NIV*).

I am unloved.

The Bible says in Romans 8:38-39, "For I am convinced that neither death nor life, neither angels nor demons, neither the present nor the future, nor any powers, neither height nor depth, nor anything else in all creation, will be able to separate us from the love of God that is in Christ Jesus our Lord" (*NIV*).

God has forgotten me.

God promises in Isaiah 41:10, "So do not fear, for I am with you; do not be dismayed, for I am your God. I will strengthen you and help you; I will uphold you with my righteous right hand" (*NIV*).

God is angry with me.

God promises in Isaiah 54:8, "With everlasting kindness, I will have compassion on you" (*NIV*).

Whatever deceit the enemy may throw our way, we can stand confident in Jesus and His Word. He is our shield, and His promises are our defense! Let's be women who believe in and rely on the Word of God, even in the midst of the greatest battle!

Steps to Awaken

What lie is the enemy attacking you with? What thoughts about yourself and God do you realize are false—deceptions the enemy has infiltrated your mind with? Write them down and then spend time in the Bible finding a few verses to act as a weapon of defense against those lies. Commit to memorizing one of the verses this week.

Day 36

It is God who arms me with strength and makes my way perfect . . .
He trains my hands for battle; my arms can bend a bow of bronze.
PSALM 18:32,34, *NIV* (EMPHASIS ADDED)

> **train**: [*treyn*] *verb*—to develop or form the habits, thoughts, or behavior by discipline and instruction: to make proficient by instruction and practice, as in some art, profession, or work.[1]

I heard one of the actors in the movie *Black Hawk Down* tell of his experiences during a TV interview. He was going to portray a Marine and so decided to spend some time with a squad of Marines before filming began. He said he had no idea what was involved in being a Marine, and he assumed that all Marines were just naturally heroic. After spending a few weeks with them, he said that what they were was *prepared*. They *trained* over and over and over again so that when they were in a battle situation they would know how to respond. Their responses became instinctual.

Heroic action is the by-product of instinct.

And instinct is developed in the unseen preparation of a warrior.

When I was training for my black belt in karate, I had to do a lot of the same moves over and over and over again. Honestly, it got a little boring at times. I didn't always see the benefit of performing the same fight moves hundreds if not thousands of times. However, as I was taking my black belt test, I found out why. The test itself was fairly grueling; and then when I was at my most exhausted, that is when the teacher told me to prepare to fight. It wasn't so much my ability or my strength . . . it was instinct developed through years of training that enabled me to fight.

It may sound boring, but if we are to be warriors, we must commit to training. This includes doing the right thing over and over and over again until it becomes habit.

Training.

We choose to forgive that person who wronged us, over and over and over again, until it becomes our instinctive response to extend love and grace.

Training.

We eat healthy meals over and over and over again before we create a healthy lifestyle for ourselves.

Training.

We go to the gym over and over and over again before we can see the few extra pounds shed.

Training.

We spend quality time with our children over and over and over again to nurture a close, loving relationship with them.

Training.

We read the Bible over and over and over again to discover God's will for our lives.

Training.

We meditate over and over and over again on the promises found in the Bible to strengthen our faith.

Training.

We pray over and over and over again to develop a personal, authentic relationship with Jesus.

Training.

I have heard it said that a thought determines an action, an action determines a habit and a habit determines our future. So what we do over and over and over again determines where we will go and how we will respond in tough times.

One of the Navy SEALs' maxims is, "Training remains strict to enforce the belief that the more you sweat in peacetime, the less you will bleed in war."

Even the Girl Scouts' motto is, "Be prepared."

If we are going to be successful warriors, we had better be prepared. And being prepared begins with training.

Steps to Awaken

Are there areas of your life where you need to begin some training? What habit must you exercise to be ready for the battles that lie ahead?

Note
1. Dictionary.com (New York: Random House, Inc., 2010), s.v. "train." http://diction ary.reference.com/browse/train.

Day 37

*Therefore, since we are surrounded by such a great cloud of witnesses,
let us throw off everything that hinders and the sin that so easily
entangles, and let us run with perseverance the race marked out for us.*

HEBREWS 12:1, *NIV*

My 19-year-old daughter, Paris, has been playing basketball since
she was five years old. I have loved watching those games (and
yelling at the refs who I am convinced all have eyesight problems!).
This year, her last year of high school, she decided to not only play
basketball but also to take up a new sport . . . cross-country.

Each race is about 5K and takes place on trails, over obstacles . . .
up hills and through the brush. It is an interesting sport . . . different for me as a spectator . . . no refs to yell at . . . and I'm not
really sure where to watch!

All the runners start off at the starting line and then take off. In
one race, the track was fairly remote, going up and down hills and
through brush.

    I was at the finish line, waiting for Paris to cross . . . and when
she did, she was crying. I rushed up to her as she was gasping for
breath and listened to her tell what had happened on part of the
trail. She told me that as she was running, she came upon a girl,
another runner, who had fallen on the track. Paris stopped to
check on her.

    The girl was hurt and wasn't moving, and when Paris asked
if she was okay, the girl whispered, "Why are you stopping? You
are not on my team." Before Paris could reply, another runner
came up to them and just jumped over the hurt girl before continuing on her way. Paris couldn't believe she had done that, and
she reassured the hurt girl, "Doesn't matter whose team you are
on, we are all runners," and then she proceeded to pick this girl
up and carry her on her back up the hill.

Eventually, Paris's coach saw her carrying the girl and came down the hill to see what was going on. He told Paris to run for the finish line and send help, because this girl had hit her head and was seriously hurt. So Paris started running again, finished her race and got help. Eventually an ambulance came to take the girl to the hospital.

In one race, Paris was elbowed in the stomach as she was running.

In another race, when the temperature was 105 degrees, she threw up as she crossed the finish line.

Initially, I thought this sport might be boring . . . boy, was I wrong!

You just never know what might happen in a race.

All the runners start out at the starting line, ready, full of hope . . . and then they are off. Anything can happen on the course—navigating the curves, the hills, coping with the heat, taking a punch in the stomach . . . and stopping to help a fallen runner.

Kind of like life.

We all start at the starting line. We are full of hope and dreams . . . and then the race starts. And now we begin navigating the curves of life, the heat, the challenges, the losses, the heartbreak . . . and the occasional punch in the stomach. As each of us are running toward our finish line, we realize that life is not a pain-free, risk-free ride.

Stay on course. Don't let the challenges cause you to quit the race that God has trusted you to run!

Steps to Awaken

Is there something in your life that is hindering you from finishing your race? What will you do about that?

Day 38

This is the only race worth running.
I've run hard right to the finish, believed all the way.
2 TIMOTHY 4:7, *THE MESSAGE*

You've all been to the stadium and seen the athletes race. Everyone runs;
one wins. Run to win. All good athletes train hard. They do it for a gold
medal that tarnishes and fades. You're after one that's gold eternally.
1 CORINTHIANS 9:24-25, *THE MESSAGE*

As the apostle Paul looked back at his life, he told his protégé
Timothy that this race of following Jesus was the only race
worth running. Basically he said, "This is the only thing worth
giving my life to." And then he challenged Timothy (and us) to
run in such a way as to win the prize. Run to win.

What does that look like?

How do we run in this "only race worth running"?

Pacing.

This race that you and I are running . . . this journey of following Jesus . . . is not a sprint. It is a marathon, and pacing is
required. Marathon runners do not run their course as if it was
a 100-meter sprint. We have to realize that we are in this spiritual race for the long haul. We don't want to fizzle out by being
a one-minute wonder. So many times, people start out with a
bang and then quit. Maybe life got hard or the obstacles got
too intense . . . or they ran out of steam, not knowing how to re-
fresh themselves in Jesus. For some reason, they quit.

Don't quit.

Just keep putting one foot in front of the other.

Handling the pain.

As most runners know, they will experience pain during a
race. Most runners will have to deal with some kind of cramp

or stitch. A runner doesn't quit the race just because of a little pain. A runner pushes through it. There is no such thing as a pain-free race. Like many others, I have had to deal with lies and the pain of a friend's betrayal. I remember telling another friend that it just hurt too much and I felt like I was trying to run my race with knives sticking in me. I remember wanting to just stop. Never mind this. I was thinking, *I don't need this kind of pain.* But that way of thinking is forgetting that the baton is the focus . . . the generations to come are the focus . . . not me. The only way the race is lost is if I sit down. We have to be careful not to abdicate the mandate that God has entrusted to us.

Don't quit.

Just keep putting one foot in front of the other.

Give the race everything you've got.

When we cross the finish line, we should have nothing left to give. We should have given everything in running our race. If a marathon runner can run another five miles after completing his marathon . . . then he did not run hard and fast enough. He should be completely spent.

Just a thought . . . If a person does not achieve his or her God-given potential, we might consider it a tragedy. We don't usually consider it sin. Maybe we should. We are not supposed to die with unrealized potential! God entrusted us with a mission . . . with a race . . . and He gave us all we need to run it and finish it.

Let's keep going!

Let's keep putting one foot in front of the other.

Steps to Awaken

What are some practical ways you can manage the pacing of your race? Have you let any pain you have experienced along the way stop you?

Day 39

Not one of these people, even though their lives of faith were exemplary, got their hands on what was promised. God had a better plan for us: that their faith and our faith would come together to make one completed whole, their lives of faith not complete apart from ours.

HEBREWS 11:39-40, *THE MESSAGE*

Unlike volleyball or basketball, most track and field events are predominantly individual endeavors. One of the exceptions is the relay race. I loved running in relay races because, while I had to do my best to run my lap with commitment and endurance, whether we won the race was not entirely up to me. I am aware though, that my performance could help my team or it could cost us the race. I was entirely responsible for the lap of the race I was running. I spent months training for my lap. I could not blame anyone else for my performance. This lap was mine. If I tripped, stepped out of the lane or got a cramp . . . the fault was mine alone. However, I found that most relay races are not won or lost in the individual laps, but rather in the baton exchange.

There are four runners in a relay race.

One starts with the baton, and one will carry it over the finish line.

As a runner is coming down the track, she is focused on one thing.

She's focused on the runner to whom she will hand the baton.

She is looking for her and her outstretched hand.

The runner waiting for the baton is running in place.

And then at a given moment, she takes off.

Not quite full speed, but definitely moving.

She is no longer looking at the runner coming toward her with the baton, she is facing forward and her hand is reaching

behind her. It is the job of the first runner to place the baton in
the outstretched hand. Once the baton is in the new runner's
hand, she then takes off at full speed. The first runner however
does not just stop on a dime . . . no . . . she continues running
behind the second runner and slowly stops . . . keeping her eyes
on her teammate.

Races are won and lost in the baton exchange.

Just ask the 2004 US Women's Olympic 4x100 relay team in
Athens . . . and the 2008 US Women's Olympic relay team in
Beijing. In 2004, the baton exchange was made out of the zone;
and in 2008, the baton was dropped. So no matter how fast and
how spectacular the individual leg of the race was, the whole
thing was lost because of the exchange between runners.

Christianity is a relay race. There are legends of faith who have
gone before us. Centuries of baton passing have kept the faith
alive. Your lap is important, but truly it is all about the baton.
It is all about the message of hope, life and truth being passed
to a new generation.

While I live *in* this moment, I am not living my life *for this moment* alone. I do have to think about the runners to come

So the reason I do my part in taking care of the planet is so that
I don't leave it a disaster for the generations to follow. It is not
always easy to recycle or buy organic, but I am trying to do my
part in leaving a clean planet for my children's children to play
in. (I'm from California—so excuse me if this sounds weird!)

The reason I take care of my body is so that I will have the
strength to pass the batons I am given.

And I need to pay attention to how I am living out my faith.
There are some questions I have asked and continue to ask my-

self: Is my faith real and genuine? Am I honest with how I do a life of faith? Does it translate to my children? Or is it just religious hype? Am I just going to church, or am I helping to build it? In thinking about the generations to come . . . am I living my life in such a way that a younger woman even wants to follow and take the baton? Am I passing on the lessons I have learned? Am I open with my life?

We walk as one . . . the legends of yesterday and the legends of tomorrow. I want to run my part of the race well.

Steps to Awaken

Ask yourself some of the above questions that I ask myself.

Day 40

THEREFORE THEN, since we are surrounded by so great a cloud of witnesses [who have borne testimony to the Truth], let us strip off and throw aside every encumbrance (unnecessary weight) and that sin which so readily (deftly and cleverly) clings to and entangles us, and let us run with patient endurance and steady and active persistence the appointed course of the race that is set before us.

HEBREWS 12:1, *AMP*

Chapter 11 in Hebrews identifies many of the legends of our faith . . . Abraham, Isaac, Moses, Sarah, Rahab, Gideon, and the list goes on. At the end of that chapter, we are told that they are joined to us by faith—"that their faith and our faith would come together to make one completed whole" (Heb. 11:40), and then Hebrews 12 begins by saying that since we are surrounded by all of these amazing legends, we should keep running the race God has set for us at this time in history.

It is now that you and I have been entrusted with God's eternal message of salvation. The generations that have gone before us have done their job. Now it is our turn. Do you feel the weight of responsibility? Do you feel privileged that we have been entrusted with this moment?

> **per·sist** [pər´sıst]—*verb*—to continue steadfastly or firmly in some state, purpose, course of action, or the like, especially in spite of opposition.[1]

Let's make a decision to throw aside any weight, and run steadily and with "active persistence" the race that God has set for us. What might be distracting you from running full on for God? What is keeping you from continuing to run with purpose?

Is it your possessions?

Are you so distracted by what you own and what you want to own that you can't run your race unencumbered?

Is it worry?

Are you worried about what the future holds? So much so, that you can't run your race free from fear?

There will always be distractions and obstacles in our path as we are running our race. We do have an enemy, and his plan is to distract us so that we don't finish our lap of this race. He wants us tired and focused on anything but running.

Let's make a decision today to run our race by keeping our eyes on the One who started us running in the first place.

Living completely sold out for Jesus is really the only way. We are not just believers, but followers. We are supposed to be living our life His way. Christianity has never been about convenience; it is always about surrendering our will to His.

Steps to Awaken

Have you gotten discouraged by life's race? What might be distracting you today from running your race?

Note

1. Dictionary.com (New York: Random House, Inc., 2010), s.v. "persist." http://dictionary.reference.com/browse/persist.

Day 41

I, Paul, am a devoted slave of Jesus Christ on assignment.
ROMANS 1:1, *THE MESSAGE*

Each person is given something to do that shows who God is:
Everyone gets in on it, everyone benefits.
1 CORINTHIANS 12:5, *THE MESSAGE*

The apostle Paul is pretty clear why he was on the planet. He was here to complete his assignment. I think it is the same for you and me.

Who are we? Devoted slaves of Jesus Christ.
What are we here to do? An assignment.
We *all* have an assignment.

As long as we are alive and breathing (I'm assuming you still are!), we have a God-assignment. We have a mission from heaven to fulfill.

I have been given a certain personality, certain gifts, talents and abilities . . . so have you . . . and this is so that we can live out our God-assignment. Rather than competing with each other, we are to each bring our strengths to the table and work together.

There are some great elite fighting forces on the earth . . . Navy SEALs, Marine Force Recon, Army Green Berets, British SAS . . . to name just a few. Members of these fighting forces are rarely deployed alone. They work together as a unit. The SEALs are often sent out in an eight-man platoon. Part of the SEAL code involves displaying loyalty to the team and teammates. They are trained to take responsibility for their own actions and the actions of their teammates.

Each member of the platoon has a different role to play within the unit. Each has a different skill, and they must learn to trust and rely on each other to fulfill their role. I doubt that they argue over who should be the medic or who should handle the communication gear. I can't imagine one of them saying, "Hey, it's my turn to be the sniper!" No. They work on letting the strengths of each member cause the unit to be stronger.

I was just thinking.

You and I have been given a mission. We have been deployed to this planet in a platoon, with more than a billion teammates. We have a mission to fulfill, so we have to get good at working together. We each have different gifts, abilities and talents in order to fulfill our purpose.

Together.

Fulfilling our God-mission will require working together.

General George S. Patton said it like this:

Every single man in this Army plays a vital role.
Don't ever let up.
Don't ever think that your job is unimportant
Every man has a job to do and he must do it.
Every man is a vital link in the great chain.[1]

Steps to Awaken

What do you think part of your God-assignment is? Have you been trying to fulfill it alone? Who is on your team who can help?

Note

1. George S. Patton, quoted in Senator Robert Torricelli, ed., *Quotations for Public Speakers* (New Brunswick, NJ: Rutgers University press, 2001), p. 259.

Day 42

*I want you to think about how all this makes you
more significant, not less. A body isn't just a single part
blown up into something huge. It's all the different-but-similar
parts arranged and functioning together. . . . But I also want you to
think about how this keeps your significance from getting blown up
into self-importance.* For no matter how significant you are,
it is only because of what you are a part of.

1 CORINTHIANS 12:14-15,19, *THE MESSAGE* (EMPHASIS ADDED)

*We each carried our own servant assignment. . . . Everything you have
and everything you are [are] sheer gifts from God. So what's the point
of all this comparing and competing? You already have all you need.*

1 CORINTHIANS 3:6; 4:8, *THE MESSAGE*

Some people can sing. I mean, *really* sing. Sing so that it touches heaven and changes hearts.

Some can dance with such style and rhythm that it is mind-boggling.

Some can take a swatch of fabric, toss it into the air, move one piece of furniture and make a room look amazing.

Some people can snap photos that make you feel as if you were there.

Some can paint . . . a room or a canvas or flowers on their nails.

Some can design clothes. Or just create a great outfit by adding a belt, scarf, necklace . . . whatever . . . I just know I wouldn't have even thought of it!

Some can make a computer do miraculous things.

Some can smile and welcome us into church or a department store . . . and they keep smiling even if we have a grumpy face.

Some can organize your closet and your life.

Some are great counselors and give excellent advice.

Some can whisper to dogs or horses.

Some can jump high and run fast.

Some can cook. Really cook. They don't even use a cook-book, and it tastes amazing. (These people are REALLY good to have on our team!)

Some people can nurse us back to health.

Some can turn a room of fifth-grade boys into well-behaved young men.

And the list goes on and on and on and on . . .

The goal is to support each other in our differences. That is what will make the platoon stronger.

Why is it that we get jealous of each other?

Makes no sense.

We are each running in our own lane. Everything I need to fulfill related to my purpose is in my lane. Every person I am to reach is in my lane. I don't need what is in your lane. You don't need what is in my lane. You and I are to discover our gifts, abilities and talents . . . many of which are in seed form . . . and then develop them. You and I are on a mission for our King. We each have our own tasks. We can't get distracted by those gifted people running next to us. We should just be glad they are on our team!

My job is NOT to resent the ability, calling or talent of my fellow platoon member . . . but rather to rejoice in who she is and what she can do.

Our platoon is stronger when each of us is running in our own lane; when each of us is growing in our own gifts and abilities.

Our platoon is weakened when we criticize each other.

When we are jealous of what we see in someone else's life.

How about if we cheer our follow runners on?

Let's encourage each other as we are running.

Not try to trip each other.

Friendly fire kills.

And we need all of us to finish strong.

Steps to Awaken

• •

Can you see that jealousy leads to criticism, which leads to division? How are we supposed to fulfill our mission if we are divided? Ask God to show you where your jealousy has separated you from your fellow platoon members. (Notice I am not asking if you have ever been jealous . . . because honestly . . . we all have!) And then list three unique abilities God has given you, and ask Him how you can use them to fulfill the mission He has given you.

Day 43

For if you forgive people their trespasses [their reckless and willful sins, leaving them, letting them go, and giving up resentment], your heavenly Father will also forgive you.
MATTHEW 6:14, *AMP*

When I saw your face, it was the face of God smiling on me.
GENESIS 33:10, *THE MESSAGE*

Because we are all a little bit weird ☺ and because we all have imperfections, we will all need forgiveness. And to receive it, we must give it.

Do you know the story of Jacob and Esau?

They were twins. Sons of Isaac.

Jacob, the second-born twin, deceived Esau and took the rights of the firstborn from him. Then Jacob ran for his life.

The two brothers basically lived separate lives apart from each other, for a number of years. By now there was the potential for a lot of bad feelings between the brothers.

One day, Jacob, who had been the deceiver, knew it was time to go home. He packed up his large family and all of his new wealth and headed home.

He was nervous. He was afraid. He had treated his brother unfairly and now was worried that his brother would kill him. He sent a messenger ahead and basically said, "Tell my master Esau this: I am coming home with lots of animals and servants, with wealth, and I am hoping for your approval. Love, your servant, Jacob."

Then Jacob prepared a present . . . lots of goats and rams, and camels and cows, bulls and donkeys. He split the herds up and put space in between them, hoping his brother would be softened by the procession of gifts. He was hoping that Esau would be glad to see him. Or if not, at least he wouldn't kill him.

Jacob had a wrestling match with God during the night and woke up having been touched by God. As he woke up, he saw Esau and 400 men coming toward him. He stood up and then bowed before his brother seven times, honoring him. He was just a little bit nervous.

But Esau ran up and embraced him . . . kissed him . . . and they both wept.

Then Jacob said upon encountering such forgiveness, "When I saw your face, it was the face of God smiling on me." Pretty amazing.

When Jacob saw forgiveness, he felt like he was seeing God's face.

Let's be quick to forgive.

Let's give someone the gift of seeing God's face.

The face of forgiveness.

Again, not saying it will be easy.

Just essential if we are going to fulfill our God-assignment.

We will not fulfill our mission alone.

We have been surrounded with people whose strengths will help bring victory.

And we need your strength to help lift the sword when someone is weary.

Our platoon is not complete without you.

Yeah, we are all a little bit weird, but we do need each other.

Together.

We.

Us.

United we stand.

Divided we fall.

Steps to Awaken

••

We all have strengths and weaknesses; sometimes someone's weaknesses can be very annoying. But if we are going to finish our God-assignment, we need to be quick to forgive. Forgive our husband and those we work with. Forgiveness is different than trust. Trust is earned, and forgiveness is freely given. As you pray . . . forgive someone that you know you need to forgive.

Day 44

*But a certain Samaritan, as he traveled along, came down
to where he was; and when he saw him, he was moved with
pity and sympathy [for him].*
LUKE 10:33, *AMP*

I stopped by a store to pick up something to eat and then headed back to my car. I walked past a homeless-looking woman who asked me for money. Without looking at her, I reached into my pocket and gave her a dollar. As I turned to get into my car, I felt God ask me to look at her. So I did. And then I smiled and said a few words to her. I realized that He just wanted me to see her as a human being with needs.

Not as a statistic.

But as one of His daughters.

I have no idea what her plans were for the money she would acquire during the day. I am not sure that is for me to judge. My job, as a Christ follower, is to keep an open heart and always err on the side of generosity, not judgment. Giving to the poor is always a good thing to do.

And truthfully, it is hard to go anywhere and not see hurting people. There are homeless people to feed, orphans and widows to care for, kids in single-parent homes, addicts in recovery. There are hurting people everywhere.

I believe we have been sent to the planet for this time in history to be the solution.

We can shut our eyes to the need or open them to be a part of the solution.

John Wesley, an evangelist from the 1700s, said: "Do all the good you can, by all the means you can, in all the ways you can, in all the places you can, at all the times you can, to all the people you can, as long as ever you can."[1]

It's time for us to awaken to care. There are needs in our neighborhoods, on our jobs, at our schools, in our families, in our own lives. Each of us has a strong desire to be known, to be seen for who we really are, so that our needs can be met in a healthy way.

Everywhere we look, there is need. However, as noted previously, there is a big difference between looking and *seeing*. When we just look, it's easy to pass by. When we see, its impossible not to act with compassion. Anybody can look, but seeing leads to action.

How can we use our lives to help the poor and the needy, the orphan and the widow, the homeless, those who are left desolate and defenseless? We can do what Jesus says in this parable.

We can stop. We can notice injustice. We can be generous with our lives by giving to other people. Not just financially. But when we share our stories, our experiences, our day-to-day lives with others, it is a comforting and consistent reminder that we are not alone. We're all in this together, and we need each other!

Leading a generous life also prompts people to open up with God, who is the Father of generosity! When we act like Him, we point people to Him. Let's be the kind of women who don't just look, but who also see the needs and then rise to meet them.

Steps to Awaken

Check out what your local church is doing in the community this week. Join them in reaching out to your city . . . Bring your whole family, or ask a friend to come along!

Note
   1. "John Wesley: Methodical Pietist," Christian History, August 8, 2008. http://www. christianitytoday.com/ch/131christians/denominationalfounders/wesley.html.

My heart is steadfast, O God, my heart is steadfast; I will sing and make music. Awake, my soul! Awake, harp and lyre! I will awaken the dawn.

PSALM 57:7-8, NIV

Well, I am not sure any of us has a harp or a lyre, but judging from the exclamation points, King David is having quite a conversation with himself! In Psalm 57, David is fleeing from King Saul, who is trying to kill him. Earlier in this psalm, David cries out to God, declaring God's refuge, love and faithfulness, reminding himself that God is above anyone else's agenda.

"Awake, my soul!" David commands himself. "Awake, harp and lyre!" David makes a decision in a very dark moment to awaken from the darkness surrounding him. He commands his soul to wake up and praise God for who He is. Yes, he knew he was on the run, but he also knew that God was his refuge. This was not David's first dark night, so he knew God would save him, as He had before.

In our darkest moments, when our circumstances look the worst, it is up to us to awaken our souls to the truth of God's Word. We have to remain steadfast to the truth. We have to remind ourselves who God is, even when the world around us tries to convince us otherwise . . .

And we can't stop there.

David says, "I will awaken the dawn." When night closes in, we must awaken the dawn—not just for ourselves, but also for those around us. We must usher in the light, causing dawn to break forth. When our lives are threatened, we must recognize that we are not alone. The enemy is smarter than to attack us one at a time . . . he wants to destroy us all. We are the light in the darkness. We must rise in dark times and allow God to shine through us to light the way for others.

Are you in the dark? Remain steadfast. Worship. Pray. Awaken the dawn with your words; and with God's light in you, shine for others to see. Awaken your soul to sing.

And if the sun is shining in your world, look for someone struggling to wait for the dawn to come. Then light up their world. We are the hands and feet of Jesus—it's up to us to remind His daughters that there is a God in heaven who loves them and that the dawn will come.

Steps to Awaken

Ask God who in your everyday life could use some light. Call her, take her for coffee and encourage her heart.

Day 46

So this is my prayer: that your love will flourish and that you will not only love much but well. Learn to love appropriately. You need to use your head and test your feelings so that your love is sincere and intelligent, not sentimental gush. Live a lover's life, circumspect and exemplary, a life Jesus will be proud of: bountiful in fruits from the soul, making Jesus Christ attractive to all, getting everyone involved in the glory and praise of God.

PHILIPPIANS 1:9-11, *THE MESSAGE*

We can use the word "love" in so many ways—connecting it with everything from the temporal to the eternal.

I love chocolate.

I love movies.

I love to read.

I love going to the beach.

I love my mother.

I love my husband.

I love helping people.

I love the orphan and the widow.

I love God.

Christians should be known as those who love. Sadly, I am not sure that we are.

Recently, I was in a small car accident. A woman turned her car into mine, and it was very clearly her fault. We both pulled over to the side of the road. I could see her talking frantically with her friend in the car. I got out the necessary documents and waited for her to come to my car.

Very nervously she asked, "Are you all right?" And then proceeded to say, "I'm sorry, it was all my fault. This is not even my car." She was just a bit panicked.

I calmly assured her that I was okay and that we could easily get this worked out. We exchanged information and then drove away.

During the next few days, I had a number of phone conversations with her as she arranged to have my car repaired. During the last conversation she asked me this question: "My friend and I have a little bet going about what you do for a living. Because you handled the whole situation with calm and were friendly, I think you must be a yoga instructor. My friend thinks you are a psychiatrist. So which is it?"

I started laughing, telling her it was neither of those, but that I was a pastor. After telling her that, there was silence. I could tell she was having a hard time believing that.

For the next few days, I thought about that conversation. It seems that Christians are better known for being critical, angry and judgmental than calm and friendly. How sad is that?

You and I should be the most grace-giving, love-filled, kind people on the planet, and yet, often that is not our reputation.

We have some work to do.

Together let's be committed to loving others. Let's let love be our reputation.

Let's not only love much, but also love well.

Steps to Awaken

Who can you love well today? A neighbor who needs help? Your husband who needs a kind word? Put action to your love.

Day 47

*Love never gives up. Love cares more for others than for self.
Love doesn't want what it doesn't have. Love doesn't strut, doesn't
have a swelled head, doesn't force itself on others, isn't always "me
first," doesn't fly off the handle, doesn't keep score of the sins of others,
doesn't revel when others grovel, takes pleasure in the flowering of
truth, puts up with anything, trusts God always, always looks for the
best, never looks back, but keeps going to the end.*

1 CORINTHIANS 13:4-8, *THE MESSAGE*

I remember the feeling when I first began to love Philip. There was this little butterfly tingly feeling inside my stomach. And I remember when I first found out that I was pregnant with each of our children. A sense of fullness filled my heart. I treasured both of those feelings. But I would like to suggest that real love is more than a feeling.

In 1 Corinthians, as Paul is describing what real love is . . . there is not one mention of a feeling. Every sentence describes an action and a decision. And every action described is to benefit someone else. Love is always about the other person.

Jesus described loving someone when He told the story of the Good Samaritan. I would imagine, as someone who did not like Jews, the Samaritan did not feel any love as he looked at the wounded, beaten Jewish man. And yet he loved him. He bandaged his wounds and paid for his care. Love. Love always involves doing, no matter what we feel.

Many churches have a mandate or motto that says something like: "Love God and love people." That really is what Christianity is all about . . . loving God and loving people. But it is much easier to say than to actually do them.

Loving people . . . those close to you and those on the other side of the world . . . means doing loving things. Forgiving. Caring. Not envying. Not demanding. Giving. Trusting. Looking for the best.

Loving God certainly involves declaring our love for Him, in songs and words. But it also goes beyond that . . . loving God involves loving people. We demonstrate our love for God by loving the people He puts in our life—those close to us and those far away.

There are many Scriptures in the Bible about caring for and loving the poor. I can't just love the poor by telling them, "I love you." That might be a nice start, but action is what is required. Which is why Philip and I sponsor children in developing nations. My saying "I love you" does not fill their bellies; but when they get a meal and know that it came from someone around the world, they feel loved.

Thousands of young women were abducted in northern Uganda and forced to become child soldiers or wives of the soldiers. All of them were brutally raped and forced to do unspeakable things. The war may be over now, but their horror is not. Many are HIV positive, and many are missing their noses, ears and lips, which were cut off as the women were trying to escape. I can tell them, "I love you." And I would imagine that feels good for them to hear. But demonstrating love by providing antiretroviral (ARV) medicine or financing reconstructive surgery to give them back their faces would be even more powerful.

Love always involves action.

Love isn't just what we feel; it is what we do, often in spite of what we are feeling.

Steps to Awaken

Read 1 Corinthians 13 in a few versions of the Bible. Write down some practical ways you can demonstrate love to the people in your immediate world and to those far away.

Day 48

Harry Houdini, the famed escape artist, issued a challenge wherever he went. He claimed he could be locked in any jail cell in the country and set himself free in short order. He always kept his promise; but one time something went wrong.

Houdini entered the jail in his street clothes; the heavy metal doors clanged shut behind him. He took from his belt a concealed piece of metal, strong and flexible, and set to work immediately. But something seemed to be unusual about this lock. For 30 minutes he worked but got nowhere. An hour passed, and still he had not opened the door. By now he was bathed in sweat and panting in exasperation, but he still could not pick the lock.

Finally, after laboring for two hours, Harry Houdini collapsed in frustration against the door he could not unlock. But when he fell against the door, it swung open! It had never been locked at all! But in his mind, it was locked, and that was all it took to keep him from opening the door and walking out of the jail cell.[1]

You and I have been set free. We have been freed from whatever thoughts or habits might be trying to keep us chained. Our job now is to walk it out . . . walk in freedom, not throw away or disregard what Jesus purchased with His blood.

Hundreds of thousands of soldiers, over a period of three centuries, have given their lives so that our nation can live free. How unintelligent would it be if, rather than living as a free nation, we decided to be in bondage to previous oppressors?

Or think of it this way: It doesn't make sense, does it, that someone who has been released from prison . . . and escorted to the gate that opens to the street and freedom . . . would turn around and go back inside?

The gates of your life have been opened.

It is time to walk free . . . free from guilt, shame, fear, insecurity, addictions, habits, unforgiveness and destructive thoughts.

So how do you do that? How do you walk free?

In many cases, walking in freedom is a process.

Part of the process involves making different decisions than you have made in the past, or else you will end up back in chains.

You have been freed, and now you must walk differently if you are going to live in freedom.

We have to realize that we can't make this journey without surrendering to God and making the decision to do life His way.

True freedom comes when we stop seeking to have our own way, and instead yield to His way. Surrendering to God is more than singing songs of surrender; it is truly letting His Word guide us. What does His Word say about fear? About habits? About sexuality? When I did life my own way, it only led me into a life of captivity; true freedom came, and continues, when I use His Word as a guide to doing life.

On this journey of freedom, during this process of transformation, there will be many times when you just have to do the right thing even though you don't feel like it. It takes awhile to create a new normal.

The journey of freedom is not an overnight one. It is not instantaneous. It will happen one day at a time as we yield to God.

Steps to Awaken

Are there areas in your life in which you need to experience freedom? Have you yielded to God in that area? What does His Word say about it?

Note

1. Zig Ziglar, quoted in James S. Hewitt, *Illustrations Unlimited* (Wheaton, IL: Tyndale House Publishers, 1988), p. 225.

Day 49

*When Jesus got out of the boat, a man with an evil spirit came
from the tombs to meet him. This man lived in the tombs, and no one
could bind him any more, not even with a chain. For he had often
been chained hand and foot, but he tore the chains apart and broke
the irons on his feet. No one was strong enough to subdue him.
Night and day among the tombs and in the hills he would cry out
and cut himself with stones. When he saw Jesus from a distance,
he ran and fell on his knees in front of him.*

MARK 5:2-6, *NIV*

Somewhere in our garage is a chunk of cement. It's not very
large. It's painted on one side with what appears to be approximately three or four colors of spray paint. For all intents and
purposes, it looks like a piece of rubble.

And that's what it is—it is rubble from what was once the
Berlin Wall (it was given to us as a gift from one of our friends
who went to Germany).

Between 1961 and 1989 the Berlin Wall stood like a prison wall
separating West Berlin (a free city with a bustling economy)
from Communist East Berlin. The Wall was built to keep the
people in Communist Germany from escaping to the freedom
of the West. And it was lined with barbed wire. Dogs and armed
guards kept watch, and gunboats patrolled the river.

One day in September 1988, a tourist on the West German side
of the wall captured on videotape a daring escape from East
Germany!

Four people, dressed in black wetsuits, were first seen leaping
from the top of the Berlin Wall. One of them, a woman, broke
her ankle in the process. They scrambled down the riverbank,

plunged into the river and swam furiously toward freedom. Onlookers on the West German side could be heard cheering them on.

Suddenly, an East German patrol boat was slicing through the waves, trying to prevent the escape. Three of the swimmers made it to shore, falling into the outstretched arms of delighted West Germans and tourists. But the fourth escapee, the woman with the broken ankle, was having difficulty.

The patrol boat bore down on her but overshot its target. Reversing its engines, the boat circled and headed again for the floundering woman. Instinctively, several men on the West German side of the river, ignoring the soldiers with guns on the deck of the patrol boat, plunged into the river and helped the woman to safety.[1]

She did whatever was necessary to get freedom.

The man described in Mark 6 was seriously bound.

So why did this man run to Jesus?
    Because he wanted freedom.
    He wanted to be free from the pain and the madness.
    And, like the woman from East Berlin, he was willing to do whatever was necessary.

I just got back from speaking at a conference in Kiev. It was awesome! There were women from Siberia who came to the conference. They spent more than a month's salary and more than 24 hours on a train because they wanted what God had for them. I was blown away by their passion to do whatever it takes. And God met them; some got miracles in their bodies; others got miracles in their hearts. God wants to do that for all of us. However, if we want what God has for us . . . a life of meaning, healing and freedom . . . then we will do whatever it takes.

Steps to Awaken

● ●

Freedom is available to us all. Are you willing to do whatever it takes to walk it out? Find three verses in the Bible about freedom and write them down.

Note

1. Jeff Strite, "Getting Your Second Wind—Which Way Will You Run?" SermonCen tral.com, September 2005. http://www.sermoncentral.com/sermons/getting-your-2nd-wind-which-way-will-you-run-jeff-strite-sermon-on-faith-vs-works-82928.asp.

Day 50

Then he said to them all: "If anyone would come after me, he must deny himself and take up his cross daily and follow me."
LUKE 9:23, *NIV*

For the first few months of my son, Jordan's, life, I remember driving the car so carefully. It was a bit scary thinking of being on the busy roads of Los Angeles with a teeny baby in the car. Most drivers on the road were not going to pay attention to the "Baby on Board' sticker I had on my window!

And yet those moments weren't as terrifying as the moment when he turned 15½ and could start driving me around. It was a scary moment when he moved from the passenger seat to the driver's seat.

I was no longer in control . . . and I like being in control.

I could stomp on my imaginary brake all I wanted (and I did that often!) but nothing happened; I was not in control.

It is a big moment in our life when we hand someone else the keys, when we trade seats; because whoever is in the driver's seat has the control. The driver chooses the destination and the speed.

Sometimes I wonder if that isn't what we say to Jesus.

"Hey, Jesus, these are my keys, and we are going my way. I want You in the car because it might be handy to have You along if I need something, like peace or joy or forgiveness, but I don't want You driving."[1]

Carrie Underwood sang about Jesus taking the wheel. And we can sing that song with her. But it is much easier to sing about Him taking the wheel than to actually give it to Him.

Because if He is driving, then I don't get to say whatever it is that I want to say. I have surrendered my words to Him. I can't just say what I want, when I want to, because He is driving. My money is not mine. I give it where He says to give it. My life is His. He is driving.

It doesn't make sense to lots of people, but real freedom comes through surrender. When we truly surrender our life to Jesus, when we make the decision to follow Him, then we experience real freedom.

Many times people think they are free, but in reality they are bound by an addiction, by unforgiveness or anger or depression or loneliness . . . and the list goes on.

The world has many people who are fans of Jesus. Fans get excited and show up when the show is on; but they often abandon the one they are a fan of when it gets hard. What the world needs is more people who are followers of Jesus—those who have surrendered their hearts, dreams and lives to follow Him. They have surrendered all to live out their God-mission, and they are walking in a freedom that is contagious.

Steps to Awaken

Does Jesus have the wheel of your life? Are there areas that you still haven't fully surrendered to Him?

Note
1. I heard a teaching from John Ortberg a few years ago in which he asked the question, "Who has the keys to your life?" That's where I got the idea for these thoughts.

Day 51

*But what happens when we live God's way? He brings gifts
into our lives, much the same way that fruit appears
in an orchard—things like affection for others, exuberance
about life, serenity. We develop a willingness to stick
with things, a sense of compassion in the heart, and a conviction
that a basic holiness permeates things and people. We find
ourselves involved in loyal commitments, not needing to force
our way in life, able to marshal and direct our energies wisely.*

GALATIANS 5:22-23, *THE MESSAGE*

There is no freedom in life until one belongs to God.

Until one decides to live life God's way.

Every other choice is an illusion.

We find the freedom to achieve the greatest desires of our heart only when we live in that relationship.

As we live life God's way, as we walk out our freedom, we will help others find freedom too.

As Jesus fulfilled His God-assignment, He went about bringing freedom. He set captives free. It started in the temporal, in what mattered in this moment . . . and then it became eternal.

One of the definitions of salvation means to deliver from difficulty . . . to give freedom.

In the Gospel of Luke, chapter 7, we learn of a woman who had been bleeding for 12 years. Sounds like agony. When she merely touched the hem of Jesus' garment, the bleeding stopped. She was set free. I don't imagine she went back to life as usual.

In the Gospel of John, chapter 8, a woman is caught in adultery. She is about to be stoned. Jesus stops the stoning and frees her. I don't imagine she went back to life as usual.

In every instance of NOW salvation with Jesus, He stopped an injustice; He stopped a sickness; He cast out a demon; He raised the dead. This was freedom demonstrated in the now.

Yes, eternity is the big issue, and it will be much longer than our time on earth. In fact, time without end. So eternal salvation is crucial; but often, NOW salvation—freedom extended in this moment—leads to eternal salvation. What opens the heart for eternal salvation are the daily acts of bringing freedom to someone.

The daily acts of liberating are what free someone from bondage so that they can fulfill their God-assignment. The woman who had been bleeding for 12 years had a purpose to fulfill; so did the woman caught in adultery. When they were freed, they could spend the rest of their lives living out their God-assignment.

A woman bound by an addiction to drugs came to a GodChicks meeting. She heard about the freedom that comes from following Jesus and truly experienced a touch from Him. She was set free. She had encountered NOW salvation.

And then the process of walking out her freedom began. She had to begin to see herself through God's eyes and begin to do life God's way. Eventually she understood that she had a God-assignment to fulfill, and so she became committed to doing that. Ten years later not only is she walking free, but she is also leading others into freedom.

And that's what it's all about.

Steps to Awaken

One of the heroes of that last story was the girl who brought the addicted woman to a GodChicks meeting. This girl knew that if she could get her friend into an environment of faith, she would encounter God. Is there someone you can take with you to church or to a Bible study or to a conference . . . and then pray that the Holy Spirit touches her heart?

Day 52

What a God we have! And how fortunate we are to have him,
this Father of our Master Jesus! Because Jesus was raised from the dead,
we've been given a brand-new life and have everything to live for,
including a future in heaven—and the future starts now!
God is keeping careful watch over us and the future. The Day is coming
when you'll have it all—life healed and whole.
1 PETER 1:3-5, *THE MESSAGE* (EMPHASIS ADDED)

Your future starts now.

To live out the life God is asking of us and to walk into the future
will require that we sow the necessary seeds TODAY. We might
need to change a few things.

In Charles Dickens's *A Christmas Carol,* as soon as Scrooge gets a
picture of his dismal future . . . he changes. He begins to sow different seeds. He becomes kind and generous. He laughs, asks for
forgiveness and reconnects with people. He changes his future.

Changing is always a choice; but if you are going to walk in the
amazing future that God has for you, change might be required.

Today's choices will affect your future.

Within the last year, I have spoken and talked to quite a few people who are frustrated because their dreams seem out of reach.
Some of them said they felt like God had spoken to them about
their future.

When talking to them, I realized that each had made some
very stupid decisions a few years in the past, and they are now living out the consequences of those decisions. A few had some mis-
demeanors on their record, and so now they can't get the job they
want. One had sex with someone she was not married to, and
now she has an STD that is life threatening. One, in a time of

stress, took a pill that eventually led to an addiction. Now this person has had to drop out of school and is now even further away from her dream. One did not listen to wise counsel in regard to finances and is now overwhelmed with debt.

This makes me so sad.

We must realize there are consequences to every decision we make.

But here's the good news!!

Don't be misled—you cannot mock the justice of God. You will always harvest what you plant (Gal. 6:7, *NLT*).

You can actually determine your future by the seeds you plant today . . . *how awesome is that???*

If there is anything in your life that you want changed, just begin to plant different seeds today!

Today is yesterday's future.

Your today is a result of the seeds you planted yesterday; and your future will look just the same tomorrow unless you begin to plant different seeds.

Your future is not about one day when . . . It is realized and worked out in now moments; all we have is this moment to plant seeds of change.

The only tool we have to change tomorrow is today.

Steps to Awaken

. . . .

What seeds can you begin to plant today that will produce the future you want? Maybe it is a future that includes being healthy. Perhaps, then, it is time to plant the seeds of eating right and exercising today. Maybe the future you want is to have a great relationship. Perhaps it is time to learn a few things about relationships. Write down some things you see in your future. What seeds are you planting to get there?

Day 53

In light of all this, here's what I want you to do.
While I'm locked up here, a prisoner for the Master, I want you to
get out there and walk—better yet, run!—on the road God called you
to travel. I don't want any of you sitting around on your hands.
EPHESIANS 4:1-2, *THE MESSAGE*

At one time or another, we have ALL been a victim of something.
From the "not so big a deal" to the "devastating."

victim (ˈvɪktɪm)—*noun*—1. a person or thing that suffers
harm, death, etc., from another or from some adverse act,
circumstance, 2. a person who is tricked or swindled; dupe.[1]

I have looked at pictures of me from the 1980s.
What was I thinking???
Definite fashion victim.
Tricked by the fashion industry into thinking those leggings
and that side ponytail looked good!
I was also a victim of thinking that I had to be like someone
else. I wasted a lot of time trying to look and act like someone else.

Many of us have been a victim of someone else's narrow mind.
Of someone's hatred.

Most of us have been a victim of some kind of discrimination.
The color of our skin. The money—or lack of it—in our bank
account. Our level of education. The wheelchair. The accent.
Our gender.
Blonde hair. (After all, you must not have a brain.)

We are all, to some degree, victims of our upbringing.
Many of us have been a victim of child abuse.
Or an alcoholic and angry parent.

Or just clueless parents who did not understand that parenting is about giving.

Maybe one of your parents died when you were young.

Maybe you were abandoned.

Maybe one of your family members was murdered.

Some of us have been the victim of a violent crime. Some of us have been the victim of a rape or mugging. There are many of us who have been the victim of a vicious disease.

I have traveled to quite a few developing nations and seen thousands of victims of absolute poverty.

Being any kind of victim is heartbreaking.

Now we must begin the sometimes long journey out.

The journey out of being a victim.

I am not saying it will be easy.

I am not saying it will be without pain.

But we can do it.

We can.

Most victims ask, "Why? Why me?"

Sometimes people get so comfortable with the title of victim that that is how they see themselves.

There will come a time when we must realize that it is time to move on.

We must choose to move from victim to survivor.

Then move from survivor to overcomer.

Steps to Awaken

Is there any part of your life in which you are still holding on to the "victim" title? Are you willing to make the journey to survivor?

Note

1. *Collins English Dictionary—Complete & Unabridged 10th Edition* (New York: HarperCollins Publishers, 2010), s.v. "victim." http://dictionary.reference.com/browse/VICTIM.

Day 54

And if the Spirit of Him Who raised up Jesus from the dead
dwells in you, [then] He Who raised up Christ Jesus from the dead
will also restore to life your mortal (short-lived, perishable)
bodies through His Spirit Who dwells in you.

ROMANS 8:11, *AMP*

sur·vive [*ser-vahyv*]—to remain or continue in existence.[1]

We have probably all sung along with Gloria Gaynor as she belted out, "I will survive!" Come on . . . admit it!

Choosing to survive takes a decision, strong motivation and courage. It takes realizing that the same Spirit that raised Jesus from the dead really does live in us!

We must choose not to let a situation or circumstance destroy us. I cried during a scene in the movie *Paradise Road* when a few of the women could no longer take their captivity. They had survived for a few years, but when moved to a new prison camp, they decided they couldn't survive another day. They just lay down on their pallets and chose to die. Survival was too hard.

So yes, it takes courage to survive.
Sometimes it takes pure guts.

Maybe you have gone through a divorce.
Yes, it was hurtful, and you wanted to stay in your bed and eat Häagen-Dazs. But you didn't. You got on with your life. You chose to survive.

Maybe a close friend betrayed you, and it broke your heart. You thought it best to just withdraw from people. But you didn't. You made another friend. You chose to survive.

You survived high school. You survived a rough patch in your marriage. A health crisis. Your child's toddler years. Their teen years. And you did it because you made a decision to.

Survival requires gaining knowledge.

To survive cancer I had to gain knowledge. I did not just yield my health to a team of doctors. *I* learned some things about health, nutrition and treatment options. *I* read books and went to seminars.

To survive troubled times in my marriage, I had to gain some knowledge. About men. About the differences between men and women. About communicating respect.

Remember, victims ask, "Why?"

Survivors ask, "What?"

What can I do to get through this?

What do I need to learn?

What should I do differently?

Surviving is good.

It means you weren't defeated.

Many of you have survived traumatic childhoods. For me, surviving cancer was good. Definitely beats the alternative!

We all might do different things to survive the situation in which we find ourselves.

We might eat chocolate . . . a lot of it.

We might cry . . . often.

We might go to a counselor.

We might hide.

All of these might be okay in order to survive.

Because we definitely want to survive.

But we will need to do things differently if we want to take the next step.

And since we are committed to running the race set before us, we *will* take the next step.

Steps to Awaken

• •

In what areas of your life have you made the journey from victim to survivor? Good job!

Note

1. Dictionary.com (New York: Random House, Inc., 2010), s.v. "survive." http://dictionary.reference.com/browse/survive.

*Yet amid all these things we are more than conquerors and
gain a surpassing victory through Him Who loved us.*
ROMANS 8:37, *AMP*

o·ver·come [*oh-ver-kuhm*]—to gain the victory; win;
conquer.[1]

We are overcomers when we are focused on helping others. We
are not concerned just about our own survival anymore. Now
we are extending our hand to someone else. We are taking what
we have learned and are using it to help another.

Honestly, this is what life is all about.

This is why we MUST move from victim to overcomer.

This is one of the most important journeys you and I will
make.

And I think God is waiting.

He is waiting for us to be able to take our eyes off of ourselves and see someone else who is hurting.

Victims ask, "Why?"

Survivors ask, "What?"

Overcomers ask "Who?" and "How?" and "Who can I help?
And how can I help them?"

Many people around the world have experienced the devastation of flooding. A lot of us, perhaps, had never understood
what a tsunami was or could do until we saw the 2004 Indian
Ocean tsunami kill more than 200,000 people. It was shocking
and heartbreaking. And I must confess, I had no idea about
what could happen to New Orleans if there was ever a breach in
the levees protecting the city from Lake Pontchartrain. But in

2005 as the waters of Hurricane Katrina pounded the city, we certainly all saw the disaster.

Many people in Southeastern Asia and New Orleans were victims of being overtaken by water.

Some survived.

They grabbed hold of a tree and hung on.

They climbed into a boat, grateful to be there.

Some were overcomers.

While they were clinging to the tree with one hand, they extended the other to bring someone else to the safety of the tree. While they were securely in the boat, they reached out and pulled others into the boat as well.

Overcomers.

Overcomers see past their victimization.

Past just "surviving." They see others who need help.

To become an overcomer, we have to realize that we were created to be overcomers.

The apostle Paul put it like this: Yet amid all these things we are *more than conquerors* and gain a surpassing victory through Him who loved us.

Amid all *what* things??

Oh just little things like . . . suffering and affliction and tribulation and calamity and distress and persecution and hunger and destitution and peril and the sword (see Rom. 8:35)!

We are more than conquerors *in* all these things . . . challenges, trials and battles. Not in spite of them . . . but in the midst of them.

In all these things.

I know some people who LOVE to surf.

They travel around the world looking for the big wave.

I have seen photos and videos of them surfing giant waves.

The kind of waves I would be afraid to swim in.

Just the photos scare me!

Yep, the surf that freaks out an ordinary swimmer like me absolutely thrills the surfer.

In the midst of the giant waves they are more than conquerors.

Steps to Awaken

The journey from victim to survivor to overcomer is not an easy one. I know. But will you commit to making it today? In whatever area of your life you need to?

Note

1. Dictionary.com (New York: Random House, 2010), s.v. "overcome." http://diction ary.reference.com/browse/overcome.

Day 56

Brethren, I do not count myself to have apprehended;
but one thing I do, forgetting those things which are behind and
reaching forward to those things which are ahead.
PHILIPPIANS 3:13, *NKJV*

On our journey toward being an overcomer, we have to set our main focus on both forgetting and reaching.

In his letter to the Philippians, Paul said that while he hadn't learned everything, he had certainly gotten good at "forgetting those things which are behind and reaching forward to those things which are ahead."

What does it mean to forget the past?

I am certainly not suggesting that we all develop amnesia. I *am* suggesting that we let go of any baggage from our yesterdays that we are dragging into our today.

Yes, you were a victim.

Yes, bad things happened to you.

Please deal with the stuff in your heart so that you can become an overcomer.

Forgive.

Let go.

You will never be able to change your past.

You will never be able to change what happened to you.

But you do have the power to create your future.

A future unhindered by the pain of yesterday.

But only if you want it.

Forgetting closes the door to your past, and reaching ahead opens the door to your future.

One time I went into a jewelry store that had two consecutive doors.

After entering the first one, I stood in a small area until the door closed behind me. The next door would not open until the first door had closed.

That's the kind of thing I'm talking about when I say you need to forget what's behind and reach ahead.

Your future is before you.

You won't enter the door of your future until you have closed the door to your past.

There are some things in all of us that must be dealt with before we can move on.

Before Paul had his encounter with Jesus, he did some terrible things. He had some forgetting to do.

Paul had to forget that on *his* orders, Stephen, a young Christian, was stoned to death while Paul stood and watched.

He was a murderer.

Could you forget that?

If Paul hadn't learned to deal with his past, he'd never have written half of the New Testament or helped establish a Church that would last millenniums.

We must put a period on the past.

The book of Joshua opens with God reminding Joshua that Moses was dead.

I am sure Joshua knew it.

In his head.

Maybe he was just a little freaked out in his heart.

So God said, "Moses is dead . . . now get up and go . . . cross the Jordan."

I just wonder.

Maybe Joshua didn't feel like he was ready for Moses' job.

He had served him for more than 40 years.

He was comfortable in that role.

Now he had to leave behind the familiar . . . why?

Because he would not have been able to lead the people into their future if he had not let go of the past.

In the past the children of Israel were nomads . . . wanderers.

In their future they were to be settlers . . . taking up residence in the land of promise.

In the past they ate daily manna.

In the future, they were to sow seeds and reap the harvests. Occupy the land.

Joshua had to let go of the past in order to walk into the future.

Steps to Awaken

• •

Are there any pieces of your past that you are not letting go of? Read 2 Corinthians 5:17. What does that verse say to you?

Day 57

*All praise to the God and Father of our Master, Jesus the Messiah!
Father of all mercy! God of all healing counsel! He comes alongside
us when we go through hard times, and before you know it, he brings
us alongside someone else who is going through hard times so that
we can be there for that person just as God was there for us.*

2 CORINTHIANS 1:3-4, *THE MESSAGE*

An overcomer is someone who uses her past to give someone else a future.

The apostle Paul told us that God comes alongside us when we go through hard times, and before we know it, He brings us alongside someone else who is going through hard times so that we can be there for that person, just as God was there for us.

Philip and I have made this journey in our marriage.

We were definitely victims . . . Philip was from a broken home and had experienced a failed marriage.

And we were just victims of trials in our own marriage.

But we made it through the challenges.

We survived. Yea!

Now we help other couples with their marriages. We teach about marriage. We have written a book together. We are determined to have a marriage that isn't just one of survival, but one that is full of life.

Overcomers.

I was a victim of cancer.

I learned some things so that I could survive.

One person told me that I really needed to live in the mountains.

Somewhere with clean air and no stress. Los Angeles does not qualify as a place with the cleanest air and least stress! And for a minute, I was tempted to pull back. But doing that would just be surviving.

And I was created to be an overcomer.

So I am determined to live in the city that God put me in and fulfill my purpose, helping people all along the way.

Overcoming always involves living *on* purpose and *with* purpose!

Don't fall into the trap of just surviving. Just getting by. You were created for more than that!

We are all trusted with the spotlight . . . big or small.

It is never so that we can just selfishly shine brighter.

But so that our light can help someone else out of the dark.

As a victim . . . you were in the dark.

As a survivor . . . you see a light at the end of the tunnel . . . so you get through.

As an overcomer . . . you become the light for someone else.

Victim.
Survivor.
Overcomer.

Who you were.
Who you are.
Who you are destined to be.

Steps to Awaken

Part of being an overcomer is coming alongside someone else who needs your strength, someone who needs to see how to get through his or her challenge. Who in your world can you come alongside?

Day 58

Now I say to you that you are Peter (which means "rock"), and upon this rock I will build my church, and all the powers of hell will not conquer it.

MATTHEW 16:18, *NLT*

Gates are not weapons.

It would be a rare thing to hear on the news that a gate killed someone.

Locked gates keep people in . . . and they keep people out.

Which is why you and I must make the journey from victim to overcomer . . . and ultimately to liberator.

As God's mobilized, unified Church, we are to reach through the gates of hell and rescue people. Those who are held captive by poverty, loneliness, injustice, fear and oppression. We have been liberated from our own fear, from our own past, and now it is our turn. Our turn to reach through the gates and bring to others the freedom that Jesus offers.

Bringing freedom to others probably won't come without a battle or two. In reality, the kingdom of God can only expand out of conflict with the kingdom of darkness.

As the children of Israel made the journey from Egypt to the edge of the Promised Land, God took care of their every need. He provided food, made sure their shoes did not wear out, gave them cloud cover in the day and a fire to bring warmth in the night. Eventually, they reached the border of what would become their new home. God could have just cleared out the land and made it easy for them to walk into it. He could have destroyed all the enemies who currently inhabited the Promised Land. The children of Israel could have moved in without the wars; but maybe God could not have made Israel the people He needed if they would not fight on His behalf.

Perhaps it is the same for you and me. Maybe we become all that God wants us to become as we wage war on His behalf . . . as we reach through the gates of hell and liberate those the enemy has bound.

Liberating someone does not have to be complicated. It can be as simple as a kind word or a hug. It can be a warm meal or a cup of water. It can be a prayer or the offer of forgiveness. Different things bind people. We have to see the need and meet it.

There is a phase that every child must grow out of.

The "all about me" phase.

This is when we are concerned with our stuff . . . our hair . . . our toys . . . our clothes . . . our agenda . . . our way.

What we have and what we don't.

Those of you with children know exactly what I am talking about. This is the time when children aren't so concerned about the needs of the whole family, just their own needs. And as parents, one of our jobs is to navigate them out of this phase.

I wonder if God isn't waiting for some of us grown-up kids to make the same journey.

We must get to the place where we realize that everything we are is meant to contribute to the mission God has sent us on.

It's not about us at all.

Again, it's about His kingdom and His cause.

Steps to Awaken

Who in your world is trapped? Is there someone who needs to be liberated—set free—in some way or another? Or is it time for you to look at the massive amount of global injustice and ask God what you can do as your part in liberating someone bound by hunger, thirst or poverty?

Day 59

*I will surely bless you and make your descendants as numerous
as the stars in the sky and as the sand on the seashore.
Your descendants will take possession of the cities of their enemies,
and through your offspring all nations on earth will be blessed,
because you have obeyed me.*

GENESIS 22:17-18, *NIV*

Abraham obeyed what God asked him to do, and then God told
him that He would bless him and his descendants. But it didn't
stop there. The descendants (including you and me) were
blessed, and now we are to be a blessing.

Abraham obeyed.

God blessed him.

God blessed his descendants.

Through the descendants the nations are blessed.

We are blessed to be a blessing.

And he [Jesus] told them this parable: "The ground of
a certain rich man produced a good crop. He thought
to himself, 'What shall I do? I have no place to store
my crops.'

"Then he said, 'This is what I'll do. I will tear down
my barns and build bigger ones, and there I will store
all my grain and my goods. And I'll say to myself, "You
have plenty of good things laid up for many years. Take
life easy; eat, drink and be merry."'

"But God said to him, 'You fool! This very night
your life will be demanded from you. Then who will get
what you have prepared for yourself?'

"This is how it will be with anyone who stores up
things for himself but is not rich toward God" (Luke
12:16-21, *NIV*).

The man in this parable had been blessed. His land had produced a good crop. And since he was rich, his land had evidently produced a few good crops. As he was looking around at all his stuff, at all his blessings, he decided that the best use of his resources was to build a bigger place to put them.

He did not give any away. He didn't think of anyone else. It was all about him.

The result? His life was demanded of him.

Definitely a sobering parable. And one that makes me think. Have there been times when, after being blessed in whatever form, I have immediately thought of how to get more or how much I could buy with what I was just blessed with, rather than wondering where I could give some of it to others?

God has no problem with you and me being blessed. He doesn't mind us living in nice homes or driving nice cars. The problem comes when we take our eyes off of the reason we have been blessed. We haven't been given stuff so that we can keep buying more stuff, but so that we can give more and more.

The book of James, chapter 1, has a few challenges for the rich. I never used to think those verses applied to me. Those verses were for the really rich ... like Oprah or Bill Gates. But then I learned a few things. So let me ask you a question.

Do you think you are rich?

The mean household income in the United States in 2009 was $52,000.[1] If we plug that number into the website www.globalrichlist.com, we will find that anyone making that much money is amongst the richest in the world. Basically, they are in the top 1 percent of the world's people. Wow.

Guess we are rich after all.

Steps to Awaken

• •

Go to www.globalrichlist.com and put in your household income. What did you find out?

Note

1. "State and County QuickFacts," U.S. Census Bureau, August 16, 2010. http://quick facts. census.gov/qfd/states/00000.html.

Day 60

Teach those who are rich in this world not to be proud and not to trust in their money, which is so unreliable. Their trust should be in God, who richly gives us all we need for our enjoyment. Tell them to use their money to do good. They should be rich in good works and generous to those in need, always being ready to share with others. *By doing this they will be storing up their treasure as a good foundation for the future so that they may experience true life.*

1 TIMOTHY 6:17-19, *NLT* (EMPHASIS ADDED)

The Bible is full of verses that let us know that God wants to prosper us. But our prosperity is not for ourselves alone.

We should be prospering in every way, because there is a hurting world that needs us to help them.

How can I help a young couple with their marriage if mine isn't prospering?

If my health isn't prosperous, how will I finish the race set before me?

If my soul isn't prospering, how can I lead others to a place of peace?

If my financial life is not prospering, how can I give to others?

The verses in 1 Timothy challenge the rich to use their money to do good . . . to be "rich in good works." And since most of us make more than $5 per day, we are rich.

I have traveled to so many developing nations and have seen abject poverty and the heartbreak that comes along with it. I have held orphans in my arms and cried along with mothers who just want help in caring for their children.

I have known people—I am sure you have too—who have a level of prosperity but use it in a stupid way. They are not making a difference in the world. They are not building anything that will last.

We are blessed to be a blessing. Period.

We are here to make a difference in the world. God put each of us on the planet . . . at this moment in history . . . so that we could use our resources to make a difference.

There is nothing in my life that I hold on to very tightly. I have come to realize over the years that all that I have is His.

When my kids were toddlers, they could be very possessive about their stuff. A friend might come over to play and reach for a toy and one of children would grab it and say, "MINE!" I would shake my head, because I had actually bought the toy, so it wasn't really theirs after all.

I wonder if sometimes we don't do that as adults . . . hold on to stuff and say, "MINE." When, actually, it is all His.

I have made a decision in the last few years . . . that I want my life to be defined by generosity. I want to be defined as a giver.

I have tithed for a long time . . . giving God back His 10 percent . . . and over the years I have consistently increased the percentage of what I give. I am not doing it to impress anyone, but simply because I want my life to be defined by generosity.

Steps to Awaken

In what area of your life can you increase your level of generosity?

Day 61

Enlarge the place of your tent, stretch your tent curtains wide,
do not hold back; lengthen your cords, strengthen your stakes.
ISAIAH 54:2, *NIV*

Enlarge.
   Stretch.
   Lengthen.
   Strengthen.
   Everything about this verse speaks of increase.
   Nothing here is about staying in our comfort zone.

Most trainers suggest that stretching is good before any workout. I know that it is a good thing to do . . . and I have suffered the consequences of exercising on unstretched muscles. But stretching hurts, so I try to ignore doing it.

For a baby to grow in the womb, it must stretch. Sometimes that is an itchy, painful process for the mother. The stretch often leaves marks.

If we are not mindful, we will settle into our comfort zone and never stretch. In the parable of the talents (see Matt. 25:14-30), Jesus rewarded the servants who stretched their talents from two to four and five to ten. The servant who just kept his one talent was severely reprimanded. God rewards the stretch.

Our comfort zone is our comfort zone because it is comfortable. (I know . . . I am really deep, aren't I?) But I would imagine that whatever is your comfort zone now was at one point some kind of stretch. I see no evidence in Scripture that we are supposed to settle in.

Each of the disciples had a comfort zone. Whether it was handling fishing nets or collecting taxes, they were comfortable doing it. Jesus invited them into the stretch. After the crucifixion, they again went back to what they were comfortable with, and again Jesus came and challenged them to stretch. Going back to what they had known and were comfortable with was no longer an option for them.

Getting married was a stretch. Having my first child was another stretch. Teaching a Bible study was a stretch. Teaching every week was another stretch. Writing a book was a stretch. Writing a book while preparing a message and traveling to speak at a conference was a bigger stretch. And now I look back at what was the first stretch, and I think, *I can't believe that was overwhelming to me!* Because now I am doing so much more. The stretch in my life has been gradual, but it has been constant.

There is a reason God is asking us to stretch and enlarge; He has more to entrust us with. He is looking for a company of people whose capacity is continuing to increase so that His purposes get done on the earth.

> *We are either progressing or retrograding all the while.*
> *There is no such thing as remaining stationary in this life.*
> JAMES FREEMAN CLARKE

Steps to Awaken

Is there an area in your life in which you might just be a bit afraid to stretch? What are you doing now that you weren't doing last year? Learning a new language? Taking a class? Volunteering at church? In what way is your capacity continuing to increase?

Day 62

But make sure that you don't get so absorbed and exhausted in taking care of all your day-by-day obligations that you lose track of the time and doze off, oblivious to God. *The night is about over, dawn is about to break. Be up and awake to what God is doing! God is putting the finishing touches on the salvation work he began when we first believed. We can't afford to waste a minute, must not squander these precious daylight hours in frivolity and indulgence, in sleeping around and dissipation, in bickering and grabbing everything in sight. Get out of bed and get dressed! Don't loiter and linger, waiting until the very last minute. Dress yourselves in Christ, and be up and about.*

ROMANS 13:11-14, *THE MESSAGE* (EMPHASIS ADDED)

Every now and then my husband and I will discover a television show we actually both like! Since we both have busy schedules, we usually TiVo episodes and watch a couple at a time when we have a chance.

It's relaxing and fun, and we get to avoid all the commercials! Woohoo!

It's easy to lose track of time when we are watching those recorded episodes. There have been a couple of times when we have sat down to watch one episode, and three episodes later found ourselves wondering if we could squeeze in just one more before heading to bed.

We had every intention of spending a certain amount of time, but ended up spending a lot more.

In life, it's easy to lose track of time. We've all been late to a party because we spent more time on our hair than we thought we would. We've all stayed out later than we planned because we lost track of time in a conversation with a friend. We've all been late to work at some point because we thought we could sleep in more than we should have.

Paul urges us in his letter to the Romans to spend our time on earth wisely. When it comes to our relationship with Jesus, we must live our day-to-day lives with purpose.

Living our lives with purpose means that we don't waste time on unrewarding pursuits.

Fighting with your spouse.
Dating a person who is not passionate about Jesus.
Dwelling on the past. Holding on to unforgiveness.
Worrying about the future.
Pursuing a career without God's direction.
Numbing pain through addiction.
Settling for mediocrity.

These are the types of time wasters we all face. They keep us from living life on purpose. They keep us from spending our time on things that will matter for all eternity.

Growing in our faith . . . spending time with our family . . . being generous and kind to those around us . . . bringing justice to those in our world who are hurting . . . introducing people to the love of Jesus . . .

These are things that matter. Our time ought to be spent on these pursuits.

We can't afford to waste the time we have been given. Jesus calls us to a far more rewarding life than one that is squandered. That life is found in relying on God's direction in our day-to-day living. When we submit our daily choices to Jesus, our life turns into a life well spent.

Steps to Awaken

Write down three things that are important to you and your relationship with Jesus. Next to each of these things, write down how you are spending time on them. Commit to one thing you can do this week to spend your time focused on pursuing these priorities.

Day 63

But make sure that you don't get so absorbed and exhausted in taking care of all your day-by-day obligations that you lose track of the time and doze off, oblivious to God. The night is about over, dawn is about to break. Be up and awake to what God is doing! God is putting the finishing touches on the salvation work he began when we first believed. We can't afford to waste a minute, must not squander these precious daylight hours in frivolity and indulgence, in sleeping around and dissipation, in bickering and grabbing everything in sight. Get out of bed and get dressed! Don't loiter and linger, waiting until the very last minute. Dress yourselves in Christ, and be up and about.
ROMANS 13:11-14, *THE MESSAGE* (EMPHASIS ADDED)

We've all heard the saying, "Dress for success."

And there's some truth to it.

I dress very differently for a baseball game with my husband than for a friend's wedding.

It would be pretty odd if I showed up in jeans and a baseball cap to a wedding. It would be even weirder if the bride at that wedding showed up wearing jeans and a baseball cap!

It probably wouldn't be the best idea to show up to the beach in the middle of summer wearing a ski jacket. It would certainly be uncomfortable!

We dress for fashion, but also for a specific occasion.

We dress with purpose in mind.

When it comes to faith, we have to dress with purpose. We have to clothe ourselves in Christ.

That doesn't mean we wear Jesus costumes, grow a beard (a scary thought) and wear sandals to work.

It means we take on the attitude that Jesus did when He walked the earth. We approach each day like Jesus did. We see each day as an opportunity to pray like Jesus did when He prayed in Matthew 6:10, "Your kingdom come, your will be done on earth as it is in heaven" (*NIV*).

What are you facing today? What do you need to dress for?

Are you facing a health battle? Dressing yourself in Christ means believing that God is your Healer.

Are you looking for work? Dressing yourself in Christ means asking for God's supernatural provision and favor.

Are you in a season of waiting? Dressing yourself in Christ means developing patience and trusting God in the season in which you find yourself.

Are you a mom to a newborn? Dressing yourself in Christ means trusting that God is leading you as a parent and strengthening you for your new role.

Dressing ourselves in Christ means that we are outfitted for whatever the day may bring. By taking on the attitude of Jesus and relying on Him, we are dressed weather-appropriate. We become ready for any storm or season that comes our way.

Steps to Awaken

What challenge or circumstance are you facing? How can you dress yourself in Christ to be prepared for that challenge or circumstance? How can you have the attitude of Jesus in preparing for today?

Day 64

Besides this you know what [a critical] hour this is,
how it is high time now for you to wake up out of your sleep
(rouse to reality). For salvation (final deliverance) is nearer
to us now than when we first believed (adhered to, trusted in,
and relied on Christ, the Messiah). The night is far gone and
the day is almost here. Let us then drop (fling away) the
works and deeds of darkness and put on the [full] armor of
light. *Let us live and conduct ourselves honorably and becomingly as
in the [open light of] day, not in reveling (carousing) and drunkenness,
not in immorality and debauchery (sensuality and licentiousness), not
in quarreling and jealousy. But clothe yourself with the Lord Jesus
Christ (the Messiah), and make no provision for [indulging] the flesh
[put a stop to thinking about the evil cravings of your physical
nature] to [gratify its] desires (lusts).*
ROMANS 13:11-14, *AMP* (EMPHASIS ADDED)

As women, we spin a lot of plates . . . And as soon as we get good
at spinning our plates, another plate gets added. Work, kids,
husband, friends . . . It can be pretty easy to get caught up in
the day-to-day obligations of life.

I don't know about you, but in the midst of all that plate spinning, it's very easy to switch on autopilot—to get to the end of
the day and ask, "Where in the world did the day go . . . and
what in the world did I do all day?!" Sometimes we are so focused on getting the job done in every area of our life that we
are unable to be present and engaged in whatever we have put
our hands to.

Unfortunately, this affects our connection to the people in our
life, and more importantly, our connection with our Creator.
How can we do life with people and miss moments or even

years in their life? Easy, we were there . . . but we weren't present—we weren't engaged. And so we miss the lives of the people around us . . . and we miss God in our seemingly insignificant day-to-day life.

Let's be honest . . . sometimes life is boring. Often, we have the false expectation that we should live for the extreme highs in life and learn to navigate the extreme lows; but in reality, most of life is spent right smack dab in the middle. The decisions we make in those times actually determine our character. Rather than switching on the autopilot (or quitting for fear of death from boredom), perhaps we could try to intentionally inject some fun, some spice, some laughter into our ordinary, everyday life instead.

This Scripture in Romans is a great reminder for us not to get so absorbed and exhausted in all our tasks that we go numb, kick into autopilot and take for granted our relationships because we are in task mode.

Relationship or friendship or ministry or work does not always come easy, particularly when it doesn't seem exciting or fun, and especially when its, well, boring. It's easy in those times to work on all the stuff we need to get done rather than work on keeping our relationship with God and people (which are the most important things!) alive and connected. It's worth the extra effort to make the boredom more enjoyable than it is to wake up a day, a year, five years later and realize we don't even know the people we see every day . . . or that we missed our God as we dozed off, oblivious to the awe and wonder He showers on us every day.

Steps to Awaken

In what area of your life have you clicked into autopilot? Marriage? Job? Your relationship with God? What can you do today to reengage that area?

Day 65

But make sure that you don't get so absorbed and exhausted in taking care of all your day-by-day obligations that you lose track of the time and doze off, oblivious to God. The night is over, dawn is about to break. Be up and awake to wake what God is doing! God is putting the finishing touches on the salvation work he began when we first believed. We can't afford to waste a minute, must not squander these precious daylight hours in frivolity and indulgence, in sleeping around and dissipation, in bickering and grabbing everything in sight. Get out of bed and get dressed! Don't loiter and linger, waiting until the very last minute. Dress yourselves in Christ, and be up and about.

ROMANS 13:11-14, *THE MESSAGE* (EMPHASIS ADDED)

Susan B. Anthony fought for the rights of women and for slavery to end. She, along with some other very brave women, desired to see women have the right to vote. And you know what?

She never saw the law come to pass in her lifetime.

That's right, she labored an entire lifetime and died 14 years before the 19th amendment giving women the right to vote was passed in 1920.

"Well, Holly," you might say, "that's a bit depressing." Perhaps, or maybe Susan B. Anthony lived knowing.

Maybe she had a bigger picture, a generational picture in mind. She kept her eye focused on the end result; and no matter what she saw . . . or didn't see . . . she believed in her heart that the world could be changed. In fact, she spent her life fighting for it . . . in the end, she was right about that risk, and the law came to pass.

Sometimes, we go through "night" seasons in our lives (and sometimes they can feel like one really LONG night). We wonder if the night will, in fact, ever be over and if dawn will ever come.

This Scripture is a promise to stand on, an encouragement to keep persevering for the bigger picture. Listen to the passion in Paul's letter to the Romans: "The night is over, dawn is about to break. Be up and awake to wake what God is doing! God is putting the finishing touches on the salvation work he began when we first believed."

Don't give up now. Don't stop doing what's right. Don't stop fighting for justice. Don't stop loving people, no matter how badly you've been hurt or betrayed. God is at work, even when we can't see His hand. He will finish what He started in each of us. We must be brave enough to choose to bank our lives on His promise. Even if that means we don't see the fulfillment of that promise in our lifetime, we can trust God's plan that includes generations. And so we can sow seeds now that will outlive our lives and benefit those who come along behind us.

Paul goes on to say, "We can't afford to waste a minute, must not squander these precious daylight hours in frivolity and indulgence, in sleeping around and dissipation, in bickering and grabbing everything in sight. Get out of bed and get dressed! Don't loiter and linger, waiting until the very last minute. Dress yourselves in Christ, and be up and about."

We do not have time to waste. James 4:14 tells us that our lives are just a vapor. This means that we have a limited amount of time here on earth. You were created with a purpose, a mission to carry out the message of God's love while you are alive. None of us can afford to spend our time frivolously, indulging our every whim. We can't spend our time focused on fighting each other, lingering on thoughts of our past or wanting all the things other people have. We can't wait until the last minute to begin our purpose . . . Your purpose starts right now, wherever you are on the journey. Begin to live your life with purpose. Let go of what is behind you and press toward what is ahead of you.

We were born for such a time as this, and there has never been a greater time to be alive . . . never has the Church had more opportunity to shine. And we shine brightest when we shine together. Time for us to get out of bed and get dressed! We must love as God loves, live—to the best of our ability—as Christ lived on the earth.

He cared for hurting people. Everywhere He went, Jesus did good. He healed the sick, comforted the brokenhearted, cast out demons from the oppressed—He fought for our rights, went to the cross and banked His whole life on the mission He was given. He was right—He won, conquering the grave for you and me to live in Him.

Now His mission is in our hands. Wake up! Let's not squander our purpose on the earth. Be up and about, living a life of purpose.

Steps to Awaken

Have you been in a long night season? Is there an area of your life that feels wasteful? What needs to change?

Day 66

She rises while it is yet night and gets [spiritual]
food for her household . . .
PROVERBS 31:15, *AMP*

This particular verse in Proverbs 31 was just a bit annoying to me for quite a while. It said that I had to rise "while it is yet night."

Whaaat??

I do my best sleeping while it is "yet night." Don't you?

But I found out that the verse has more to say than just the time of day we get up, and has everything to do with being someone who "rises" in the midst of hard times. When darkness and chaos abound . . . when others might be apathetic . . . we rise.

I think our world is looking and waiting for a company of people who will rise in the midst of hard times. It would be so much easier to sit . . . to give in, to give up.

I know.

We have all felt like that.

But we are supposed to be the ones rising.

The rising that we must do starts on the inside.

King David and his army returned home one time to find out that the enemy had not only invaded their home but had also taken their wives and children.

> David and his men burst out in loud wails—wept and wept until they were exhausted with weeping. David's two wives, Ahinoam of Jezreel and Abigail widow of Nabal of Carmel, had been taken prisoner along with the rest. And suddenly David was in even worse trouble.

There was talk among the men, bitter over the loss of
their families, of stoning him. David strengthened himself with trust in his God (1 Sam. 30:4-6, *THE MESSAGE*).

It makes me feel good (in a sick sort of way ☺) that the first response of David and his men on encountering such a loss was
that they cried until they could cry no more. Tears were one of my
initial responses to the diagnosis of cancer five years ago. I cried
until I was exhausted.

Have you been there?

Have you suffered such a loss . . . or heartbreak . . . that you
wept until you had no more tears?

Not only was David heartbroken at his loss, but also his friends
were blaming him. They wanted to kill him. This was not a pretty
situation.

But David did something that should be an encouragement
to us.

He got up.

He was knocked down and overwhelmed on the outside. But
on the inside he rose. He strengthened himself by looking to God
rather than his loss.

Then he rallied his army. Together they recovered their families and all they had lost.

I just think we can't sit around and wait for God to change
our circumstances. We have to first rise on the inside, trusting
that our God wants to deliver us.

There was a time when my marriage was at a "not good" place. I
wanted to lie down and whine, in fact I might have, but eventually I made the decision to rise.

There have been times in parenting when I have wanted to lie
down . . . but I make the decision to rise.

There have been times when it would be easier to give up on a friendship, to just lie down, but I make the decision to rise.

Steps to Awaken

Is there an area of your life where you are sitting down when you need to rise? Is it time right now to rise? Can you trust God with that area?

Day 67

The voice of the LORD is powerful; the voice of the LORD is majestic.
PSALM 29:4, *NIV*

In Joshua 1, the children of Israel are at a critical point in history. After 40 years of wandering the desert, God is giving the Israelites a second chance to enter the land of promise.

Many of us are positioned to enter what He has promised us.

A future filled with hope.

A heart full of peace.

A body healed.

Provision for our needs.

As we are positioned to enter His promise, we have to be able to hear His voice.

The book of Joshua opens with God talking. It's not surprising that God was speaking. He always does. What is surprising is that Joshua listened.

I think Joshua learned to hear the voice of God from watching Moses. He learned to value the voice of God.

Amazing things happen when we listen to God.

God reminded Joshua in the first chapter that Moses was dead, and that it was up to Joshua to lead the people into their future. Joshua had to let go of the past and listen to God's voice.

God told him, "I will give you every place where you set your foot . . . No one will be able to stand up against you all the days of your life. As I was with Moses, so I will be with you; I will never leave you nor forsake you" (Josh. 1:3,5, *NIV*).

I was in a hospital for a couple of weeks and heard lots of doctors' reports. I was learning about all the changes I would need to make in the future to maintain my health. It was a little overwhelming. Then one morning very early, all was quiet, and I heard a whisper from heaven . . . His whisper . . . and it made all the difference . . . "I am with you . . . be strong, Holly."

It is in God that I found my strength . . . and so will you . . . He is saying the same thing to you.

The apostle Paul learned this. When he wrote his second letter to the Corinthians, he told them (and us) that he found strength in his own weaknesses. Because when he was weak, then God showed His strength.

Joshua's time in listening to the voice of God gave him the ability and authority to lead the people into the Promised Land. They crossed the Jordan and entered their future.

I am not sure where you are today. Maybe you are feeling weak and afraid, unsure of the next step to take on your journey. Or maybe you are feeling strong and sure. Either way, His voice will help you.

Hearing His voice is not hard. Open your Bible and begin to read it. His Word is His voice. Let it bring strength and encouragement to you.

Steps to Awaken

Read Joshua 1. Can you hear the voice of God speaking to you?

Day 68

Every part of Scripture is God-breathed and useful one way or another—showing us truth, exposing our rebellion, correcting our mistakes, training us to live God's way. Through the Word we are put together and shaped up for the tasks God has for us.

2 TIMOTHY 3:16, *THE MESSAGE*

When I was a five-year-old, I won a prize for regularly attending Sunday School. It was a little white Bible with a zipper around it. I couldn't even read that Bible, yet I loved it.

While I was at Duke University, I took many different Bible classes. I enjoyed studying the history of the books of the Bible and learning all about the people. I read through parts of the Bible many times for those classes. And mainly because I wanted an *A* on the exams!

In those days, I am not sure I really understood the power of God's Word. Now I read the Bible for a different reason.

It is like a map.

A map can show you the roads to take to reach your destination.

On our lifelong mission trip, the future is unknown and the Bible is our map.

The Bible is filled with stories. It is filled with adventure and poetry, and in it is the greatest wisdom for all time. When I read the Bible, I certainly appreciate the stories; *but* I read it with an open heart so that it will change me . . . strengthen me . . . energize me . . . equip me.

I read through the book of Proverbs often, and I read it by reading one chapter a day. As I was reading chapter 18, I came upon this verse:

Answering before listening is both stupid and rude (Prov. 18:13, *THE MESSAGE*).

Hmmmm. Now, I can just read this and quickly move to the next verse, or I can ask myself, *Have I done this?* And the answer is yes! Well, because I don't want to be known as stupid or rude, I will ask the Holy Spirit to help me be a better listener.

> I love you, LORD; you are my strength. The LORD is my rock, my fortress, and my savior; my God is my rock, in whom I find protection. He is my shield, the power that saves me, and my place of safety (Ps. 18:1-2, *NLT*).

Again, I can just race through this, or I can let it speak to me. I am not a journaler (pretty sure that is not a word!), but often I will write down Scriptures that speak to me, and I wrote this one down. I listed all the qualities describing God from this verse: Strength, Rock, Fortress, Savior, Shield, Protector, Safety. In the middle of challenge, or uncertainty, He is all those.

A few weeks ago, I had to have a routine MRI. From the beginning of my cancer diagnosis five years ago, MRIs are one of my annual exams. For this particular MRI the nurse injects a substance into my veins so that the image is made clearer. On this particular day, it took four tries to find a vein that would work. OUCH!! And at one moment, the smell of the room and the solution took me back to the original diagnosis, and I started to feel fear. There was no reason . . . I am doing great . . . I was just taken back. And it is in these kinds of moments when we must let His Word be more than information. This is the moment when I had to say to God, "You are my rock, my safety, my protector!"

Steps to Awaken

Read Psalm 119. Write down some of the verses that describe the Word of God.

Day 69

The Lord is my Rock, my Fortress, and my Deliverer; my God, my keen and firm Strength in Whom I will trust and take refuge, my Shield, and the Horn of my salvation, my High Tower. I will call upon the Lord, Who is to be praised; so shall I be saved from my enemies.
PSALM 18:2-3, AMP

I recently came across this quote on warfare written more than 2,500 years ago:

> If you know the enemy and know yourself, you need not fear the result of a hundred battles. If you know yourself, but not the enemy, for every victory gained you will also suffer a defeat. If you know neither the enemy nor yourself, you will succumb in every battle (Sun Tzu).[1]

The truth in these words still speaks to you and me today.

In battle we must know ourselves and we must know our enemy.

Every coach talks to his or her team about the opposing team before the game. Often the team will watch films of previous games or go see the other team play someone else. Why? So that they can learn the strategy of their "enemy." And if they know how their "enemy" plays, then they can adjust their game accordingly.

You and I do have an enemy. (And it is not an opposing basketball team!) Our enemy is not merely a man dressed in red and holding a pitchfork. He is far more than some sort of supernatural boogeyman birthed out of age-old superstitions and fables.

The enemy is Satan, who opposes God and will stop at nothing to see those whom God loves—which is all of humanity—suffer in darkness and despair. The enemy's intent is to keep us eternally separated from the love of God.

The enemy uses deception and lies to prey on our weaknesses. In the battles we face, the enemy specializes in deceit to stop us from experiencing the love, freedom and victory that we have in Jesus.

We know our enemy, but we don't need to fear him.

Why? . . . Because we also know ourselves.

We know who we are in Christ.

We can withstand the attacks of the enemy simply because we know to whom we belong. We are daughters of the King, children of God. In the midst of great battles, we find victory in God's strength!

He is our Rock, which means He is our steady ground in the midst of turbulent times!

He is our Fortress, which means that when things get tough we can find shelter in God's love and kindness!

He is our Deliverer, which means that when we call out to God, He hears us and will come to our rescue!

He is our Strength, which means that we can receive comfort and energy from Him when we are tired or overwhelmed!

He is our Shield, which means that He protects us with truth from the lies of the enemy!

He is the Horn of our salvation, which means that He saves us and leads us to safety!

He is our High Tower, which means that He can give us a proper perspective on the battles we are currently facing!

In whatever challenge we find ourselves, in whatever battle we awaken to, we need not fear the result of a hundred battles. We gain victory in knowing that our God, in whom we find our strength, is much greater than our enemy!

Steps to Awaken

Read Psalm 18:2-3 a couple times out loud. Spend five minutes thanking God for who He is and the strength He has given you!

Note

1. Sun Tzu, *The Art of War*, book 3, c. 500 B.C., as quoted in Giles, trans., *Greenhill Dictionary* (London: Greenhill Books, 2006), p. 502.

Day 70

·····•‿✦‿••·✧·•❦•·✧·••‿✦‿•·····

But those who wait for the Lord [who expect, look for, and hope in Him]
shall change and renew their strength and power; they shall lift their
wings and mount up [close to God] as eagles [mount up to the sun]; they
shall run and not be weary, they shall walk and not faint or become tired.
ISAIAH 40:31, *AMP* (EMPHASIS ADDED)

The truth is that most of us don't like waiting. When we want
something . . . we want it now!

Our great-great-great-great-grandparents, when they wanted dinner, had to grow it or catch it and then cook it over an open fire.
This took hours. Lots of waiting. And now we pace in front of the
microwave frustrated that it is taking 45 seconds!

I don't even like to wait for you to finish your sentences . . . I'd just
as soon finish them for you!

Every day is filled with those little moments of waiting that test
our patience and our nerves.

On another level, we wait for a promotion or for a goal to be realized, for a dream to be fulfilled, for our body to get stronger or
for a relationship to be reconciled. There are lots of waiting moments in life.

What can we do while we are waiting? While we are waiting for an
answer to prayer or while we are waiting to understand?

We can keep growing and learning . . . with expectancy!

Gary Preston tells a story in his book *Character Forged from Con-*
flict that illustrates how we are to wait. He writes:

Back when the telegraph was the fastest means of long-distance communication, there was a story, about a young man who applied for a job as a Morse code operator. Answering an ad in the newspaper, he went to the address that was listed. When he arrived, he entered a large, noisy office. In the background a telegraph clacked away.

A sign on the receptionist's counter instructed job applicants to fill out a form and wait until they were summoned to enter the inner office. The young man completed his form and sat down with seven other waiting applicants. After a few minutes, the young man stood up, crossed the room to the door of the inner office, and walked right in. Naturally the other applicants perked up, wondering what was going on. Why had this man been so bold?

They muttered among themselves that they hadn't heard any summons yet. They took more than a little satisfaction in assuming the young man who went into the office would be reprimanded for his presumption and summarily disqualified for the job. Within a few minutes the young man emerged from the inner office escorted by the interviewer, who announced to the other applicants, "Gentlemen, thank you very much for coming, but the job has been filled by this young man."

The other applicants began grumbling to each other, and then one spoke up, "Wait a minute! I don't understand. He was the last one to come in, and we never even got a chance to be interviewed. Yet he got the job. That's not fair." The employer responded, "All the time you've been sitting here, the telegraph has been ticking out the following message in Morse code: 'If you understand this message, then come right in. The job is yours.' None of you heard it or understood it. This young man did. So the job is his."[1]

The young man got the job because he was not just waiting—all of the other men were waiting too—but he was waiting expectantly. We might all be sitting in the waiting room. But it is how we wait, and what we do with the waiting, that is important. The young man in that office was listening. And because he was, he was rewarded. Waiting does not mean just sitting down and doing nothing.

As a young girl, I certainly had a dream of having a great marriage. And today . . . I do. But it wasn't because I said "I do" 25 years ago and then just sat around in my wedding dress, with my eyes closed and waiting for it to be great. No. I had some learning to do. I had some work to do. The waiting involved some learning along the way.

Steps to Awaken

What are you waiting for? And are you waiting with expectancy? Are you learning? Are you growing?

Note

1. Gary D. Preston, *Character Forged from Conflict: Staying Connected to God During Controversy* (Minneapolis, MN: Bethany House Publishers, 1999), p. 117.

Day 71

One Saturday morning 15 years ago, I decided to have a garage sale. Philip and Jordan were off riding horses, and I was setting up the sale. Paris, who was almost three, was roaming around the front yard "helping" as only a toddler can.

A neighbor came over, leading her newly acquired dog on a leash. Paris went to pet the dog, when suddenly the dog turned and bit Paris in the face two times before his owner could stop him. With blood pouring down her face, Paris started screaming and running toward me. I scooped her up, realizing this would require more than Band-Aids, put her in her car seat and we made the quick dash to the emergency room.

Upon arriving, the nurse told me that a plastic surgeon happened to be on call. This was good news. Definitely a good thing to have a plastic surgeon put stitches in a face!

As the surgeon was preparing, I had to hold Paris down as he injected shots of Novocaine in her face to numb it so that he could begin stitching her up. In her little raspy, weepy voice, as they were giving her shot after shot, Paris told me, "Mommy, I am okay . . . I want to go home now." So did I! But we had some work to do first.

Holding my daughter down while she was bleeding, in pain, getting shots and more than 40 stitches WAS THE HARDEST THING I HAVE EVER DONE. But it never occurred to me to let someone else hold her down.

So in that moment I was brave.

As a side note, when I got her home, she asked where the dog was because she thought he needed a spanking!

The life that you and I have been given will include moments that absolutely require us to be brave.

Courage is one of the qualities God demands of us as we face the unknown future. Just like Joshua.

In the first chapter of Joshua, God tells Joshua (and us) four times to be courageous. Why? Could it be because He knew we wouldn't likely get it the first time? Is it because God knows our courage is sometimes hard to hold on to?

One of the definitions of courage implies facing the difficulties ahead with enthusiasm. Wow. Not sure I would go that far. I am up for facing challenges . . . but usually it is because it is necessary . . . not because I am looking forward to it.

Since God is asking us to be courageous, we must be able to!

It is not like He is asking us to be seven feet tall. He is asking or, rather, commanding us to be something that He has equipped us to be.

God calls us, just like He called Joshua, to take *our* land . . . whatever that would be . . . marriage, job, parenting, health . . . with strength and courage.

We need courage as we live out our God-adventure.

We'll need courage in order to speak up when it is necessary. We'll need courage to navigate a health challenge.

We'll need courage to get through a rough time in a marriage. We'll need courage to forgive the person who betrays us.

Steps to Awaken

Read Joshua 1. What situation in your life today will require you to have courage?

Day 72

Take the thousand and give it to the one who risked the most.
And get rid of this "play-it-safe" who won't go out on a limb.
Throw him out into utter darkness.
MATTHEW 25:28, *THE MESSAGE*

The life God is asking you and me to live will involve risk and stepping into the unknown.

It did for all of the Bible heroes.

In the book of Genesis, God told Abram to leave his home—Ur—which, according to some scholars, was the most highly developed city of the ancient world. He left to pursue what God had for him, which ultimately involved bringing blessing to all the people on earth. However, all of the details of what would come were unknown to him.

God just said, "Go."

And Abram did.

What if he had stayed back in Ur? I would imagine he had a nice, safe life in Ur. He probably had all he needed. If he had, we wouldn't even know his name, and we would not have the blessing that his obedience has brought us.

In the last few years, I have gotten some emails from women all over the world who are struggling with a lack of motivation, inspiration or just a feeling of "blahness."

Perhaps many of you who are reading this have become Christ followers. You have made your peace with God. Your hearts are healed. You have been set free. Your marriages are getting stronger. You have received comfort and healing on the journey. You are learning to walk in wisdom . . . NOW WHAT??

Don't think I've come to make life cozy (Matt. 10:34,
THE MESSAGE).

If Jesus told us that He did not come to give us a cozy life . . .
then why do we continually look for one? Perhaps in some people's minds the American dream involves getting settled behind
a white picket fence, having 2.2 kids and money in the savings
account. While we can certainly have our white picket fence,
our children and our savings account, I just don't think settling into a life of coziness should be our goal.

In many of us there might and should be divine restlessness.
Perhaps we are thinking, *There has got to be more to life than this!*
     And you are right!
     Our life is not supposed to be like the movie *Groundhog
Day*—just doing the same thing over and over. Some level of
risk and adventure is required!

I am not necessarily talking about risking your life! I'm not taking about jumping out of a plane or bungee jumping off a
bridge. These activities certainly would be considered risking
your life, and feel free to do that if you must! (Personally, I am
not jumping out of a perfectly good airplane!) But in a way,
those are easier and often require less courage than forgiving a
friend who has betrayed you or staying married through a hard
patch . . . or parenting a teenager.

What would be a risk for you?

Asking someone to church? Going on an overseas missions
trip? Writing a bigger than normal check to give to a charity?
Feeding a homeless person? Learning to drive a car? Volunteering with youth? Enrolling in university?

Whatever it is . . . do it today. Jesus did not come to give us a
cozy, sit-back life of comfort. He called us to change the world.
And that will take risk!

Steps to Awaken

• •

What does this verse in Matthew say to you?

> Meanwhile, the eleven disciples were on their way to
> Galilee, headed for the mountain Jesus had set for their
> reunion. The moment they saw him they worshiped
> him. Some, though, held back, not sure about worship,
> about risking themselves totally (Matt. 28:16, *THE
> MESSAGE*).

Day 73

The Lord God is my Strength, my personal bravery, and my invincible
army; He makes my feet like hinds' feet and will make me to walk [not
to stand still in terror, but to walk] and make [spiritual] progress upon
my high places [of trouble, suffering, or responsibility]!

HABAKKUK 3:19, *AMP*

I believe that I have been sent to the planet at this time in history
to fulfill a plan that God has. My life is not my own. It is His.

He is my personal bravery.

He is my invincible army.

And because He is both of those, He will cause me to walk . . .
not stand still in terror . . . but to walk. Which means I can't allow myself to get overwhelmed with whatever obstacle might be
in front of me.

I am very aware that is much easier said than done.

Some of us are taking care of aging parents.

Some of us have special-needs children.

Some of us are facing a battery of medical tests.

Some of us are handling staggering financial challenges.

Some of us have lost a job.

Some of us just don't know the next step to take.

Whatever the challenge, He is our personal bravery. And when He
actually is our strength and bravery, then He will make us walk . . .
not freak out . . . but walk. And not only walk . . . but also to make
progress in our areas of trouble and suffering.

And responsibility.

I love that the verse in Habakkuk uses the word "responsibility."
Not a very glamorous word. But somehow reassuring.

Some of us get up day after day and go to the same job and do the same thing.

Some of us daily take care of children and we wonder if we will ever have an adult conversation.

Some of us go to school every day and perhaps are wondering where it will lead.

Some of us wake up and look at the same man that we have for the last 30 years.

As you and I are walking daily in the places where reliability and dependability are demanded of us . . . God will meet us. He will be our personal bravery so that we can make progress . . . not only in the big areas of challenge and suffering . . . but in the daily, mundane, possibly boring areas of responsibility.

Whatever we face . . . trouble, suffering . . . or the everyday-ness of responsibility, He is our personal bravery.

Steps to Awaken

Read Habakkuk 3:17-18. In the midst of challenge, Habakkuk still exalted His God. Now, you may not be depending on fig trees and flocks in the field, but what are you facing? And how can you determine to exalt your God in the midst of it?

Day 74

*Consider it pure joy, my brothers, whenever you face trials of
many kinds, because you know that the testing of your faith develops
perseverance.* Perseverance must finish its work so that you
may be mature and complete, not lacking anything.

JAMES 1:2-4, *NIV* (EMPHASIS ADDED)

This is one of those verses that have been a challenge for me.
Because my first response to any trial is not joy.

As Christ followers, the goal of our walk with Jesus should
be maturity. We should be growing up . . . and this verse tells us
that maturity does not come from how much we know but from
how much we persevere. And perseverance is not developed in
the good times . . . it is produced in the moments of challenge.

I have never needed to persevere through a massage or a shoe-
shopping excursion. ☺ Perseverance is only necessary and is developed as we get through the situations that don't come easy.

In Mark 6, right after Jesus and His disciples had fed at least
5,000 people with a couple of tuna sandwiches, verse 45 tells us
that Jesus insisted that His disciples get in a boat and go to the
other side of the lake. The word that is translated "insisted" actually means forced. Jesus forced His disciples to get in the boat
without Him and go to the other side.

Makes me think that maybe there was something in this little
boat ride that the disciples were going to need to face.

While they were rowing for the other side, we read that they
were having a hard time. Perhaps it got stormy or windy. Maybe
they were afraid. I am sure they began wondering, *What are we
doing here? This is too hard! It was way more fun back there feeding all*

those people. Why do we have to go to the other side? This is hard. Why did Jesus send us here anyway?

Now comes my favorite part. Jesus, who doesn't always use a boat, began to cross to the other side by walking on water. He saw His disciples straining at the oars, and Mark 6:48 tells us that He would have walked by them. I love that. He saw His disciples wrestling with the wind and waves and would have just kept right on walking. At first when the disciples saw Jesus, they cried out, afraid . . . until they realized who it was. (I am not sure who else they thought would be walking on water.) They called out to Jesus, and then He got in their boat, calming the wind and the waves.

I think Jesus knew that the disciples had everything they needed within them to get to the other side . . . after all, He was the one who sent them there. They were in His will. And yet, when the journey got hard, all they had to do was call on His name and He would get in their boat.

I am certainly not perfect (a loud AMEN from my friends!), but to the best of my ability I am living my life in the will of God. I was rowing my little boat when suddenly five years ago a storm of cancer came. As I was "rowing" through this storm, I often thought, *Hey, I liked it better back there . . . where there was no pain, and surgery wasn't needed.*

And yet, the road with God is always ahead.

I did know that He had given me all I needed to get to my shore; and I did know that all I needed to do was call on His name and His presence would flood my soul.

He will get in your boat too.

As you are persevering through your storm, and you feel like the wind and the waves of your circumstance are overwhelming, you can call on Him. His presence will bring peace to your soul so that you can persevere and get to your "other side."

Steps to Awaken

Read Mark 6. Interesting, huh?

Day 75

*But Ruth replied, "Don't ask me to leave you and turn back.
Wherever you go, I will go; wherever you live, I will live. Your people
will be my people, and your God will be my God. Wherever you die,
I will die, and there I will be buried. May the* LORD *punish me severely
if I allow anything but death to separate us!" When Naomi* saw that
Ruth was determined to go with her, *she said nothing more.*
RUTH 1:16-18, *NLT* (EMPHASIS ADDED)

The book of Ruth tells us a great story.

A woman named Naomi is married to Elimelech. They are
Israelites but are living in Moab, a foreign land filled with people who don't know the God of Israel. For some reason, Elimelech and his two sons die. Naomi decides that she wants to go
back home to Bethlehem. She tells her two daughters-in-law,
Orpah and Ruth, of her plans, and encourages them to stay in
their home, Moab.

Both of them tell Naomi that they would rather go with
her, and so the three of them set out on their journey.

I would imagine that it was a hard trip. They had each just
lost their husbands, and so I am sure it was difficult emotionally. And then it was physically challenging and perhaps even
dangerous, especially for three women. At one point along the
journey, they come to a crossroads.

The road less traveled is before them.

Naomi again pleads with both Orpah and Ruth to go back
to Moab.

Orpah looked at the uncertain road ahead, and said, "Okay,
I do think I will return to Moab."

Moab was certainly the more familiar.

So Naomi kissed Orpah and sent her back to the land of
her past.

But Ruth refused to go back.

Her determination to continue this journey was evident to Naomi, so Naomi quit asking Ruth to return to Moab.

Determination is more than a feeling. It is more than a wish. It is more than a promise.

Determination can be seen. It can be seen in our everyday actions.

And I think determination is what is missing so often today.

In finishing a course at school.

In building a marriage.

In parenting.

In staying on a diet.

In seeking God.

All of these require determination in order to be successful.

I have realized that many times God does not ask us to do something hard . . . just impossible!

One-hundred-year-old Sarah having a baby is not hard . . . it is impossible . . . but with God it becomes possible!

Staying married and loving that man is not hard . . . it is impossible (at least some days it feels like it!) . . . but with God it becomes possible.

The opposite of determination is being complacent or disinterested.

When you and I stop walking passionately and with determination on the path God has for us, we begin to get complacent. And complacent people will never accomplish what God has entrusted them with.

Ruth's determination to stay connected to Naomi eventually led her to a marriage with Boaz, which put her in the lineage of Jesus.

We need to be a company of determined women . . . pushing through and refusing to back off the God-assigned path! Our determination will affect generations.

Steps to Awaken

In what area of your life do you need to demonstrate determination? What do you think the result will be if you don't? (And if you haven't read the book of Ruth, set some time aside to do that!)

Day 76

But Ruth replied, "Don't ask me to leave you and turn back.
Wherever you go, I will go; wherever you live, I will live.
Your people will be my people, and your God will be
my God. Wherever you die, I will die, and there I will be
buried. May the LORD *punish me severely if I allow anything*
but death to separate us!" When Naomi saw that Ruth was
determined to go with her, she said nothing more.
RUTH 1:16-18, *NLT* (EMPHASIS ADDED)

This is a verse about relationships.

Most of us know about the importance of having a relationship with God. Everything else in life springs up out of our God-encounter.

And most of us would understand the importance of having a strong, passionate, committed relationship with our husband.

But this verse (which is often read at weddings) is about a friendship. And more than just a casual friendship, it is a covenant . . . a forever one.

Ruth is making a powerful statement. Thousands of years later, you and I know the amazing end of Ruth's story, and how her commitment to Naomi was essential in all that would come her way. But in this moment she had no idea of the future ahead of her. It was a risk.

She made a determination to spend the rest of her life wherever Naomi was.

One of the phrases around our church that has become foundational is "doing life with each other." This means we don't just come to church on Sunday and then do the rest of our life alone. No, we have baby showers. We are present at each others' births and deaths. We drive hours to have dinner together. We pray for each other. We laugh and cry together. We don't always agree, but we forgive each other and make it through the hard times together.

The people you and I do life with will in many ways determine the course of our life. In our very transient culture, staying connected with people might be difficult . . . but it is so worth it. I have some women in my life that I have committed to forever. That means, no matter where they live, what season of life they are in or the challenges we face, I will do the work to stay connected. I have given these people permission to speak into my life. To challenge me when I need it and to hold me accountable to God's call on my life. This means that to them . . . my life is an open book. Yes, it is risky. Because they see the not-so-good parts of me. But I can't imagine doing my life without them.

Steps to Awaken

Do you have any forever, covenant girlfriends? Are there some that you might need to reconnect with today?

Set up road signs; put up guideposts.
Mark well the path by which you came.
JEREMIAH 31:21, *NLT*

In 1803, Lewis and Clark were two explorers who were sent out by President Thomas Jefferson to find a waterway connecting the Atlantic Ocean to the Pacific Ocean. They were given money to fund their journey. They used the money to buy food and supplies, but what seemed a bit unusual was how much money was spent on ink. Many may have questioned that purchase because "that ink wasn't critical for making the trip, but it was critical to make the expedition a success by recording its findings."[1]

It is necessary to mark the trail.

Lewis's expedition journals were invaluable. He drew pictures of the animals and plants he encountered. He used the ink to draw maps. He recorded every detail in his journals. There is a difference between making a trip and marking a trail.

Think of Jeremiah 31:21 in journey terms.

We are all on a journey.

We will all face stormy moments along this journey. When we are in the middle of a storm, we have a decision to make. We will either move forward, determined to stay on the path, or we will quit.

The journey of a marriage will take determination. The start is always fun! And then the occasional dry, rough patches come.

Maybe some hard, seemingly uphill, times.

We are ALL going to have challenging, stormy moments in our marriage.

Philip and I had some rough moments in the early years of our marriage. Of course they were all his fault! But we didn't give up. We got help. We read books. We went to marriage seminars. We talked to Jesus, and were just determined to build a strong marriage. Now almost 26 years later, our marriage is in such a sweet place. And honestly, it would have been so easy to lose determination along the way.

(I do want to clarify something. If you are being abused in your marriage, get out and please get help. I am not asking or even encouraging you to stay in a marriage where you are being abused.)

Most marriages end with what has been called "irreconcilable differences." We all have those. It takes determination to work them out.

Being diagnosed with cancer was certainly another storm in my life!

You and I can't always ask, "Why? Why did this happen? Why am I in this storm?"

But we can answer *how*.

How will I navigate this part of my journey? And what kind of trail am I marking that others can follow?

I have an obligation as a Christ follower to navigate this path well . . . not perfectly . . . but with determination. Not only for me, but because there are others who will be coming along on this path and watching to see how to navigate it.

I navigated the challenges in my marriage, not perfectly, but to the best of my ability . . . because I knew that there is a generation coming up behind me who needed to see how a couple builds a marriage.

I navigated the challenges of cancer, not perfectly, but to the best of my ability . . . because, sadly, there will be other women walking this path who will need to see how someone navigated the storm.

There are others following behind *you*; they are watching to see how to navigate the journey of being a college student, an executive or a working mom. There are those following you who need to see how to navigate loss . . . or even favor. We each have the responsibility to mark well the path we have walked.

Steps to Awaken

Who in your life is looking to you to see how you are navigating life's challenges? Are you marking the path well so they can follow?

Note
1. Stephen E. Ambrose, *Undaunted Courage* (New York: Touchstone, 1996).

Day 78

Be strong and courageous, do not be afraid or tremble at them, for the LORD your God is the one who goes with you. He will not fail you or forsake you.
DEUTERONOMY 31:6, *NASB*

The Hebrew word for "fail" is *raphah*. This word has many meanings in the Old Testament. It can mean to let go, to let drop or to sink down, to abandon, to let alone. In other places it is translated as idle or to slacken or dishearten, to faint in the day of adversity.

I love this.

God promises not to let go of us or allow us to sink, not to abandon us or leave us alone. He is not idle, and He is a very present help in our day of adversity.

Yes . . . *this* is your day to be courageous. This is your day to make progress on places of trouble, suffering and responsibility (see Hab. 3:19). This is your day to take bold steps. This is your day to take a deep breath and confidently take the next step on your journey. But the great thing is . . . YOU ARE NOT ALONE!!

Your God will NOT fail you. Ever.

He is there in our moments of challenge and adversity, and He will not fail or forsake us. With His strength to back us, we can be courageous. All we have to do is take the first step; our success does not depend on our ability, but on the presence of the King of the Angel-Armies.

Sometimes people think that the sign of God's blessing is a life with no challenges. I don't think so. I think that could mean we are not courageously taking steps and getting involved in the life He is leading us in.

We are certainly free to sit behind our white picket fence, relishing our comfortable life; or we can get out of the boat and take some risks, trusting that our God will never fail us. The promise is that He will be with us as we *go*.

Esther could have kept her mouth shut.

Ruth could have stayed in Moab.

Deborah could have decided not to join the battle.

Mother Teresa could have continued her comfortable life in Albania.

Jim Elliot did not have to be a part of the mission to reach the Waodani people.

David could have kept the stones for his sling in his pocket.

Noah did not have to build an ark.

Moses could have stayed in the backside of the desert.

Accepting the challenge and obeying the leading of our God is always a choice.

All I know is that my life would be safe and boring if I had not stepped into the adventure God had for me.

And I know that, regardless of whatever challenge comes, He will not fail or abandon me. What a promise!!

Steps to Awaken

Is there something . . . some kind of adventure . . . that God is holding before you? Maybe it is forgiving someone? Or maybe it is talking to your neighbor? Or taking a class? Or maybe it is going on a mission trip? Do you confidently know that as you embark on whatever journey it is . . . He will not fail you?!

Day 79

The lines of purpose in your lives never grow slack,
tightly tied as they are to your future in heaven, kept taut by hope.
COLOSSIANS 1:5, *THE MESSAGE*

Jonathan Edwards said that those who think most about the life to come . . . about eternity . . . actually make the greatest impact in this one.

So really . . . those who are heavenly minded do the most earthly good!

You and I need to live this life knowing that it is connected to our eternal future. Sometimes in our very materialistic, gratification-seeking, temporal world it is easy to lose sight of the eternal.

We can't really separate our earthly future from our eternal one. They are definitely connected. What we do with this tiny slice of eternity affects the rest.

In each of the parables in Matthew 25, Jesus makes the point that our present actions determine our eternal future.

The first parable is about the ten virgins waiting for the bridegroom. They all took their lamps to wait for him, but five were foolish and unprepared, not living expectantly, even though they knew the bridegroom was coming. They squandered their lives and their time and weren't ready. They didn't have oil for their lamps, so they didn't get to join the party. We can't be squandering our lives, living as if Jesus is not coming back.

The second parable is the parable of the talents. Three servants were each given different amounts of money by their master to manage while he was gone. They each had the freedom to use what their master had entrusted to them. When the master came back, two of the servants had multiplied what he had given them, and the master rejoiced, telling them to enter his joy. One servant simply returned the original. The master was angry with the one who did nothing with what he had been given, and so was cast away into outer darkness. You and I have been entrusted with talents and resources here on earth that we are supposed to be using and multiplying in ways that honor God.

The last parable is perhaps the most confrontational. Jesus will come back and separate people into two groups—the sheep and the goats. Sheep are the ones who gave water, food and clothes to those in need. Sheep are those who invited strangers into their lives and visited those in prison. Jesus said that when they did all this, it was as if they were doing it for Him. The sheep will be blessed by God and enter the Kingdom prepared for them since before the creation of the world. On the other hand, the goats are those who did not give to those who had need. And Jesus said that by refusing to bring help and love where it was needed, it was as if they had refused Him. The goats get sent away to eternal punishment. This does not sound like a good place to get sent! Taking care of the hurting and the hungry, the lonely and the thirsty is our responsibility. And when we do that, it is as if we are loving Jesus.

All three of these parables tell us that our actions in this life affect our future. How we wait for Jesus, how we manage what He has entrusted to us, and how we care for people matters.

So it seems that what we are doing for "the least of these" not only affects their earthly future . . . but it seems to affect our eternity.

Steps to Awaken

Read Matthew 25. What does it say to you?

Day 80

*Your life is a journey you must travel with a deep consciousness of God.
It cost God plenty to get you out of that dead-end, empty-headed life you
grew up in. He paid with Christ's sacred blood, you know. He died like
an unblemished, sacrificial lamb. And this was no afterthought. Even
though it has only lately—at the end of the ages—become public knowledge,
God always knew he was going to do this for you. It's because of this
sacrificed Messiah, whom God then raised from the dead and glorified,
that you trust God, that you know you have a future in God.*

1 PETER 1:18-21, *THE MESSAGE* (EMPHASIS ADDED)

If you close one eye, hold out your thumb and move it toward
your eyes, it seems as if your thumb can cover up much larger ob-
jects than itself.

That is the power of perspective.

Because your thumb is so much closer and immediate, it appears
bigger than larger things in the far distance. Which isn't the truth.

It's really a matter of perspective, because what is beyond is much
bigger than your thumb.

Often we tend to focus on the here and now, our immediate con-
cerns, letting them overwhelm and dominate, and they block out
larger and longer-term considerations.

While we live in this moment . . . we are not living FOR this moment . . . we are living for eternity.

> Time on earth . . . short.
> Eternity . . . long.

I am not sure that I gave my eternal future in heaven much
thought until I was diagnosed with cancer.

The truth that earth time is short and eternity is long became very real to me; and while I am doing great (five years cancer free!), the reality is that none of us knows how many days on the earth are allotted to us.

At some point, I will cross from this life and step into eternity. Because I have put my faith in Jesus . . . I will enter heaven . . . *my true home* . . . and experience all that that could be.

Pure joy . . . unending parties and celebration . . . reunion with loved ones . . . complete freedom from every pain and sorrow. I will experience perfect love, because I will be in the presence of Jesus.

And there will also be a time when, in heaven, I will give an account for my life . . . for all that I did for my God and King on the earth.

I know that . . . so that motivates me . . . motivates me to tell people about the love and forgiveness of Jesus . . . so that they, too, can experience heaven . . . and motivates me to give to the hungry and the thirsty, to love the orphan and the widow . . . and motivates me to live a life that honors Him.

Knowing that eternity is what matters . . . I look at the challenges on earth differently.

We can't always choose the circumstances we will walk through, but we can choose how . . . by keeping eternity in our hearts.

When we realize that our time on earth is to make full use of what God has given us . . . it will make a huge difference in how we live our lives.

Steps to Awaken

How do thoughts of heaven make you feel?

Day 81

Do justice to the weak (poor) and fatherless;
maintain the rights of the afflicted and needy.
PSALM 82:3, AMP

She was spit upon, ridiculed, laughed at and scorned.

She was called a witch and a baby killer.

Everywhere she turned, she faced repeated rejection.

She lost the man she loved.

He, like most men of their generation, did not want a woman who had opinions and thought for herself. He was attracted to and at the same time repulsed by her intelligence.

She was severely injured and became blind in one eye.

She was a woman who courageously pioneered her way into an arena solely occupied by men.

If it had not been for a desperate plea from a dying friend and a supernatural divine revelation from God, she would surely have quit. But she didn't quit.

Instead, against all odds, Elizabeth Blackwell accomplished her dream. In 1847, she entered medical school and became America's first woman doctor.

She accomplished her dream by courageously focusing on *why* she was becoming a doctor.

At that time in history, poor women virtually had no health care.

Many died.

She was determined to change that.

So when she was ridiculed, when she felt fear from the threats of others, she tapped into the courage we have all been given and made the decision to rise.

Today, women of all generations have a lot to applaud Elizabeth Blackwell for.[1]

At different seasons of life, and as we rise up to bring justice where we see injustice, we will all be faced with fear.

Overcoming fear is our biggest battle.

Lots of people ask . . . what if I mess up? What if I fail? And so the fear of failure keeps them from trying.

But I say . . . is there not a cause??

But for this cause came I unto this hour (John 12:27, *KJV*).

When talking about His upcoming crucifixion, Jesus told His disciples that He wasn't trying to get out of it. But instead He was born for this moment. To lay down His life for them . . . and for us.

This is your moment. Let the cause always be bigger than your fear or the obstacles.

The cause of bringing justice.

The cause of helping the poor.

The cause of building your marriage.

The cause of finishing school.

The cause of_____.

Steps to Awaken

Fill in the last blank in the list above.

Note

1. Holly Wagner, *GodChicks* (Nashville, TN: Thomas Nelson, 2003), pp. 36-37.

Day 82

Rescue the perishing; don't hesitate to step in and help.
If you say, "Hey, that's none of my business," will that get you off
the hook? Someone is watching you closely, you know—Someone
not impressed with weak excuses.
PROVERBS 24:11-12, *THE MESSAGE*

Sometimes it is fear that can cause us to draw back from our mission to execute justice.

And sometimes it is indifference.
Indifference to what is going on around us.
Indifference to the hurting.
Indifference to the needs of people.
We are not supposed to be indifferent to what is going on in our world.

We might say, "Oh, I am going to rest . . . take a break."
That is fine.
We just have to be honest with ourselves and admit it when taking a break turns into sitting out the battle.

Jesus was not very impressed with anything lukewarm.
And when we enter into the lukewarm danger zone, we find that we don't care much about anything. Not hurting people. Not lost people.
And not the mission for which we were created.
So be careful.

Being content is good. Content with today. Content with what we have.
But I don't think being satisfied is ever good. Being satisfied can lead to slowing down, which can lead to stopping, which can lead to lukewarmness.

Not good.

I think the opposite of indifference, of lukewarmness, is passion.

Being indifferent, being passive, can get us in trouble.

King David found this out.

One spring, a time when all kings were supposed to be in battle, David decided to stay home.

And then he just lazed around in bed all day.

When he arose in the evening, he saw a beautiful woman taking a bath.

She was Bathsheba.

And most of us know the end of that story.

Could it be that his passivity when he should have been at war opened the door to temptation, which led to adultery and murder?

We had seen David be courageous and passionate as he ran toward Goliath and as he led his troop of "mighty men."

And yet, like all of us, when he backed off and let indifference to the cause of His God take over, trouble came.

We all have a mission in life, a God-assignment.

We can't ever forget that.

We can't be indifferent to it.

And it will take passion to complete it.

Steps to Awaken

Is there an area of your life in which you started out passionate but now find yourself indifferent? Maybe disappointment or a sense of hopelessness has taken over. If this area is a part of your God-assignment, then can I please ask you to pray? Pray for a sense of purpose to overtake the indifference.

Day 83

But my servant Caleb—this is a different story. He has a different spirit; he follows me passionately. I'll bring him into the land that he scouted and his children will inherit it.

NUMBERS 14:24, *THE MESSAGE*

Before every major battle, the commanders motivate their troops with passion. They remind them of the cause and the reason they are in this fight. No warrior casually heads into battle.

It is passion that stirs up the "fight" in all of us.

I have seen many people lose battles simply because the fight has gone out of them.

I have seen people fighting illness who simply yielded.

I am not judging.

I know how tiring it can be to fight disease.

But cancer is not a casual disease.

It is an aggressive monster.

And it must be fought with passion and aggression.

Passion is contagious.

Passion motivates.

Left alone, most things will settle at average.

Including marriage.

If we want a great marriage, we are going to have to fight for it.

And that will require passion.

I am not just talking about sex. Although that is certainly important! (And fun.)

I am talking about passionately learning, forgiving, trying.

As soon as we back off, our marriage can settle at average . . . and then the downward spiral begins.

Reaching a dream requires passion.

Sitting on the couch for hours watching television instead of actively pursuing your dream is not going to bring the results you want.

Sitting on the bleachers, spectating, while others pursue their dreams will only bring frustration.

Just hoping your dreams come to pass is not going to do it.

You will need a plan.

And you will need to stir up the passion within you to reach it.

Fulfilling your purpose will require passion.

The passion to overcome obstacles.

The passion to persevere.

It will take passion to reach the finish line and hear, "Well done."

Bringing justice will require passion.

The passion to not only see the need, but do something about it.

The passion to rally your friends into making a difference.

It will take passion to keep His cause first and foremost.

It will take passion to make His name famous.

In a scene from *Return of the King*, the third in the *Lord of the Rings* trilogy, Aragorn tries to inspire his outnumbered men against what seems like sure defeat. Hell's swarming legions have gathered before them, and the courage of Aragorn's fighters is weakening. Riding along the front lines of his discouraged army, he shouts:

> I see in your eyes the same fear that would take the heart of me. A day may come when the courage of men fails, when we forsake our friends and break all bonds of fellowship. But it is not this day . . . THIS DAY WE FIGHT!

Steps to Awaken

In what area of your life have you lost passion? What can you do about it? Is there an area related to bringing justice to our world that you are passionate about? Who knows it?

Day 84

But a certain Samaritan, as he traveled along, came down to where he was; and when he saw him, he was moved with pity and sympathy [for him], and went to him and dressed his wounds, pouring on [them] oil and wine. Then he set him on his own beast and brought him to an inn and took care of him.

Interruptions.

So many times we feel frustrated by interruptions.

They are distractions.

There have been times when I have been trying to work, and one of my children would want to talk.

Times when I was reading a good book and my husband came in the room.

Times when I was well on the way to finishing my to-do list when my phone rang.

Some of these interruptions can be hindrances to finishing my assignment; but some of these intrusions could be . . . a divine interruption.

A nudge from the Holy Spirit that is unexpected.

A whisper from God.

Some of the great miracles of Jesus occurred when He was interrupted.

A man being lowered through the roof interrupted His teaching.

A woman touching the hem of His garment interrupted His walk.

A man crying out to Him, "Have mercy on me!"

The Pharisees asking Him, "Shouldn't this woman be stoned to death?"

So many interruptions.

But He was always available. How about you?

Are you available? Is it possible that God is in that interruption?

The Good Samaritan allowed his journey to be interrupted that day—and Jesus noticed. Jesus told us that the way the Samaritan took care of the hurting man is the way we should demonstrate love to our neighbor. This is the second and highest command in the universe.

He stopped and got involved.

He paid the bill. He nursed the wound. He cared for the injured man.

Sometimes it's easy to say a short prayer for the hurting. It's easy to ask someone else to help.

But maybe some things should not be delegated.

How many times have we thought, *Somebody should do something about that*... Maybe we are the someone. Maybe the reason we are even noticing that something needs to be done is because it is our assignment.

What have you noticed in the last week . . . that maybe . . . just maybe . . . God was using to try to get your attention?

Is there someone you can help today?

Steps to Awaken

Keep your eyes open today for some God-interruptions!

Day 85

Defend the poor and fatherless; do justice to the afflicted and needy.

PSALM 82:3, *NKJV*

de·fend [*dih-fend*]—verb—to ward off attack from; guard against assault or injury; protect.[1]

As a mother, protecting and defending my children is instinctive and second nature to me. I can think of countless times when I've had to protect them from injury.

When Jordan and Paris were young, I would try to protect them from falling off their bikes and scraping their knees. And I can remember warding off an attack from bees, protecting my children from stings.

I'm sure we can all think of a time we've had to defend a loved one—when we've had to come to someone's aid when they were in need. Sometimes it's as easy as keeping a watchful eye or speaking out on someone's behalf. One time I stood up for a friend as someone started saying mean things to her. I just put a stop to it. She began to call me her knight in pink armor. Ha!

But many times we might have to go a step beyond speech to defend.

I know we all are willing to do this for someone we love, but what are we willing to do for someone we don't know?

Around the world there are literally millions of orphans. According to UNICEF and UNIAIDS, approximately 47.5 million orphans live in Sub-Saharan Africa (and that's just a portion of Africa); 2.5 million of them live in Uganda. I read in fact that every 15 seconds a child becomes an orphan.[2] Pretty staggering, isn't it?

These are children who are alone and left without anyone to defend them.

While the statistics may be overwhelming when you think in terms of the whole, each "1" represents a child who needs to be protected—from disease, from hunger . . . and so many other horrible things.

My dear friends Marilyn and Gary Skinner, founders of Watoto Ministries in Uganda (Watoto.com), rescue vulnerable children and women daily. They not only feed and protect them physically, but emotionally and spiritually as well; they provide them with hope and a new chance at life. They decided what they were willing to do for people in need they didn't know. Now, thanks to their efforts over the years, thousands of women and children have been rescued . . . but the Skinners didn't start by rescuing thousands; they started by rescuing one.

We all have people in our world who need to be protected . . . defended . . . rescued . . . It may look different for each of us, but we each have someone in our path—and within our reach—who needs us to defend and protect them.

Steps to Awaken

In addition to your family, what one person in your world can you reach out to and help? Take a moment today to go out of your way to help someone in need. Don't know where to start? It's easy—just start with one act of kindness or sign up to volunteer with a local charity. And remember—you don't have to rescue the millions; just start by helping the one!

Notes

1. Dictionary.com (New York: Random House, Inc., 2010), s.v. "defend." http://dictionary.reference.com/browse/defend.
2. "Orphan Statistics," Habitat for Humanity, www.hfgf.org/statistics.pdf.

Day 86

God's Spirit is on me; he's chosen me to preach the Message of good news to the poor, sent me to announce pardon to prisoners and recovery of sight to the blind, to set the burdened and battered free, to announce, "This is God's year to act!"

LUKE 4:18-19, *THE MESSAGE*

Years ago, there was a TV show called *The Doris Day Show*. Its theme song included the words *"Que sera, sera . . . whatever will be, will be . . ."* It might have been a catchy tune, but the fatalistic attitude behind it can bring trouble.

Some statistics say that there could be 50 million orphans in Africa in the next few years if we don't do anything.

50 million.[1]

And right now around the globe there are 27 million people who have been abducted and sold into human slavery.[2]

27 million.

Every 15 seconds somewhere in the world a child dies from a water-related disease.[3]

15 seconds.

And this year, in the United States alone, 200,000 marriages will end before their second anniversary.[4]

All horribly tragic statistics, so I can't just be singing *"Que sera, sera"*!

No. I have an obligation to bring change to the future.

And if I am going to bring change, then I must fight for it. You and I were entrusted with this moment in history not to sit idly by or get depressed about all that is unjust but rather to be a part of the solution.

> For we are God's workmanship, created in Christ Jesus
> to do good works, which God prepared in advance for
> us to do (Eph. 2:10, *NIV*).

There are good works God has prepared for you to do.

It certainly involves people and situations in your immediate world. The single mom who needs groceries or just a listening ear.

The college student in your neighborhood who needs help with a class.

The foster child who needs a home.

Your husband who needs to feel respected.

And, I think God has prepared good works for us to do that involve helping the poorest of the poor around the world. Whether you ever get on a plane and go to a developing nation or not, you can get involved. (Although I do think that it would be great if everyone could truly see what abject poverty looks like.)

We can all pray.

We could sponsor a child who desperately needs our help. (www.godchicks.com . . . Social Justice tab . . .)

We could get some of our friends together and fund the building of a water well in a community where children are dying from water-related diseases (www.generositywater.org).

We could partner with A21 to help abolish human trafficking (www.A21.org).

We could support one of the thousands of women whose lives and faces have been destroyed by the LRA in northern Uganda (www.Watoto.org).

We could write a letter to a Christian who has been imprisoned for his or her faith. It still happens all over the world (www.voiceofthemartyrs.org).

There are many more . . . you pick. Just do something. We were entrusted with this time in history for a reason. Let's make a difference!

Steps to Awaken

• •

Check out the websites I've listed. Is there one that God might be leading you to get involved with?

Notes

1. "The Experiences of Family Caregivers Concerning Their Care of HIV/AIDS Orphans," *South African Family Practice*, 2009; no. 51, vol. 6, pp. 506-511. http://www.indexmedicus.afro.who.int/iah/fulltext/.../Experiences%20of%20family.pdf.
2. "What's the Story?" Free the Slaves. http://www.freetheslaves.net/Page.aspx?pid=301.
3. "Goal: Ensure Environmental Sustainability," Unicef Millennium Development Goals, http://www.unicef.org/mdg/environment.html.
4. Findings based on a nationwide study of 455 newlyweds and 75 longer-married people looking back on their first year of marriage. Published in Miriam Around and Samuel L. Parker, *The First Year of Marriage.* http://lovetakestime.com/art-sev enquestionstoask.html.

Day 87

I don't know about you, but I'm running hard for the finish line.
I'm giving it everything I've got. No sloppy living for me! I'm staying
alert and in top condition. I'm not going to get caught napping,
telling everyone else all about it and then missing out myself.
1 CORINTHIANS 9:26, *THE MESSAGE*

A friend of mine used to run track years ago in high school. She competed in long-distance races.

Long-distance running. Yuck. ☺

Her coach used to tell her that more races were lost by distraction than by speed. In longer races, the runner must maintain focus at all costs. When a runner forgets even for a minute that the goal is to reach the finish line first, the runner forfeits any chance at winning.

Why? When a runner forgets why she is running, she loses sight of her pacing and falls behind.

Life is the same way, isn't it?

We were meant to win the race that God has laid out for our life.

And we all know that life isn't a sprint; it's more like a marathon. There will be many legs to our race.

There will be different seasons, and we will learn how to run in both the sunshine and the storms that come our way. At times we will feel like we were born to run; the feeling of moving forward and taking new steps will feel exciting and adventurous.

Other times, we may feel so tired, with feet hurting and endurance waning, that all we want to do is quit.

It's important that we remember there is a reason for the run. We are running for an eternal prize. The pace, the focus and the determination in which we run have eternal implications. The message and love of Jesus will spread with every step we take. Justice is delivered to the hurting and the oppressed with every lap we diligently run.

Distractions come in many forms . . .

When we compare ourselves to the person running in the lane next to us, we become distracted.

When we focus on our emotions and our pain more than the finish line, we become distracted.

When we begin to dream about the ease and comfort of the spectators around us, we become distracted.

And when we fail to see the obstruction up ahead, we become more than just distracted—we become injured!

First Corinthians 9:26 reminds us that the real focus of our race is not on the conditions we find ourselves running in or even what the race will demand of us.

Our real focus is on Jesus.

We run toward Jesus through prayer, through reading the Bible, through being an active part of our local church . . .

. . . And when we run toward Jesus, we run to win.

Steps to Awaken

Read 2 Timothy 2:1-7. Ask yourself, *What is one thing I can do this week to run to win? How can I eliminate distractions in my life and focus on developing a stronger relationship with Jesus?*

*"Don't be afraid," the prophet answered. "Those who are
with us are more than those who are with them." And Elisha
prayed, "O LORD, open his eyes so he may see." Then the LORD
opened the servant's eyes, and he looked and saw the hills full of
horses and chariots of fire all around Elisha.*

2 KINGS 6:16-17, NIV

Opening our spiritual eyes so that we can see the promises and
protection of God should probably be something we all pray for!
So many times we see the obstacles rather than what God might
be doing for us.

In the book of Numbers, chapter 13, God told Moses to send
out 12 spies to check out the land He had promised to give
them. Two of the spies, Joshua and Caleb, came back after scout-
ing the land and basically said something like, "Moses, we are
well able to take the land! We saw a great place! Yes, there are giants, but, man, you should see the size of the grapes!" Joshua
and Caleb weren't naïve; they saw the challenges, but they just
saw God as bigger!

Ten of the spies came back and said, "No way can we do this!
There are giants, and they are too big. We are just grasshoppers."

They saw themselves as grasshoppers.
Why?
Maybe because they had been in slavery for 400 years. They
had a slave mindset and saw themselves as bugs.

I don't think God could have let them enter the land in that condition. They would have been destroyed.

So they spent 40 years wandering around the desert, learning
how to trust God. Perhaps some were learning how to see
through His eyes. God waited for those bound by a slave mind-

set to die off so that He could let the ones willing to see the promise enter in.

Years later, Joshua sent out two spies to check out Jericho. And they came back, saying, "Yes! God has given us the country." They were a different generation with different eyes and a different spirit.

How do you see yourself? As able to possess the promise of God . . . or as a bug?

The grasshopper mentality says:
    "I'll never make it in life."
    "I am a single mom and have been abused and abandoned, and my dreams will never come to pass."
    "My marriage is too far gone."
    "I am in too much debt."
    "I don't deserve the good life."

We have to begin to see ourselves as God sees us!
    Winners.
    Overcomers.
    He wants us to leave our mark on the world; and we can only do it by seeing ourselves through His eyes. There is much work for you and me to do at this time in history. There are giants in the land. Giants of injustice and poverty. We can let them freak us out or we can realize that we were born for this!

We have the ability to change how we see what we see.
    We may not be able to change what we see, but we can determine how we are going to see it.

Steps to Awaken

• •

Is there a circumstance in your life that seems so big that you just don't know how you can get through it? Is it possible that you could begin to change how you see yourself? Is there anything "bug-like" in your thinking? ☺

Day 89

People are watching us as we stay at our post,
alertly, unswervingly . . . in hard times, tough times, bad times;
when we're beaten up, jailed, and mobbed; working hard, working
late, working without eating; with pure heart, clear head, steady
hand; in gentleness, holiness, and honest love; when we're telling the
truth, and when God's showing his power; when we're doing our best
setting things right; when we're praised, and when we're blamed;
slandered, and honored; true to our word, though distrusted; ignored
by the world, but recognized by God; terrifically alive, though
rumored to be dead; beaten within an inch of our lives, but refusing to
die; immersed in tears, yet always filled with deep joy; living on
handouts, yet enriching many; having nothing, having it all.
2 CORINTHIANS 6:3-10, *THE MESSAGE*
(EMPHASIS ADDED)

Harriet's life was not an easy one.

She was born into slavery in 1820, and suffered greatly at the hands of her owners.

In 1850, she escaped into Canada, but she didn't rest there.

From 1851 until the end of the Civil War, she helped rescue more than 300 slaves and see them safely delivered to Canada.

Time and time again, she herself went back into the South, risking capture and certain death every time.

Because she wanted as many people freed as possible.

Countless numbers owe their lives to her.[1]

Thank you, Harriet Tubman, for staying at your post.

I don't know to which posts you have been assigned, but I am suggesting that you stay at them.

One of my posts is as a *wife*. So, even if Philip and I have a serious disagreement, and I am not a happy camper and Mr. Universe walks by quoting Shakespeare, I'm not going to follow him home! I know that my post is next to Philip forever.

Another of my posts is as a *mother,* so I have spent time training my children and loving them, even though there are times when I wanted to send them far, far away! I am committed to that post.

Another of my posts is as a *teacher,* so I spend time training my mind, going to conferences and studying so that I can continually improve.

I am also a *friend,* so I invest time in people, even perhaps when I'd rather be alone. I am doing my best to stay at the posts to which I have been assigned.

My main post is *believer.*

In the midst of the battle, can I still believe in the goodness of God? When enemies surround me, can I still worship my God? Or do I blame Him? Can I remain a faithful believer?

Jehoshaphat, king of Judah, was surrounded by a bunch of enemies who all wanted to destroy him. I imagine it was terrifying.

But he did an amazing thing.

He didn't get angry with God.

He didn't ask why.

Before they planned to march into battle, he bowed down and worshiped God. He then appointed a choir for God who were to march ahead of the troops.

A choir.

The praise team.

He didn't put the guys with the swords in front.

He put the worship leaders.

Guess he was serious about his post as a believer . . . as a worshiper.

While they worshiped, God set ambushes, and the enemies were destroyed.

Can you stay at your post as *believer in* the midst of your battle?

As we bring justice to a world that is crying out for it, we will encounter battles. The enemy is not going to surrender his ground easily. Please don't give up. Don't walk away. If we all stay at our posts, victory is ours!

Steps to Awaken

To what posts have you been assigned?

Note

1. "Harret Tubman Home," New York History Net. http://www.nyhistory.com/har riettubman/.